Committee of Vigilance
The San Francisco Chamber of Commerce Law and Order Committee, 1916–1919

A Case Study in Official Hysteria

by
Steven C. Levi

McFarland & Company, Inc., Publishers
Jefferson, North Carolina, and London
1983

Letter from Older to Phelan quoted by permission of the Bancroft Library, University of California, Berkeley.

Greater San Francisco Chamber of Commerce Minutes and Papers, selected papers and letters of the League of Women Voters, and selected papers and letters of James R. Rolph, Jr., quoted herein are by permission of the California Historical Society, San Francisco.

Photographs of Frederick J. Koster, the July 1916 Chamber of Commerce mass meeting, and the October 1916 page of *The Argonaut* are all reproduced by permission of the California Historical Society, San Francisco.

Library of Congress Cataloging in Publication Data

Levi, Steven C.
  Committee of Vigilance.

  Bibliography: p.
  Includes index.
  1. San Francisco Chamber of Commerce. Law and Order Committee. 2. Strikes and lockouts — California — San Francisco — History — 20th century. 3. Open and closed shop — California — San Francisco — History — 20th century.
  I. Title.
  HD5326.S4L48 1982   363.2′09794′61   82-17302

ISBN 0-89950-058-7

© 1983 Steven C. Levi. All rights reserved.

Manufactured in the United States of America

Acknowledgments

In the process of writing this book I found myself indebted to many people and institutions whose assistance I can never repay. A special thanks must go to Peter Evans of the California Historical Library in San Francisco. Without his helping hand this book would never have become a reality. Also thanks to Larry Englemann, Robert Levinson, Donald Swain, and my parents and friends who have read more rough drafts than it is humanly possible to count.

Of the libraries I used special thanks must go to the Bancroft Library, the Huntington Library and the California Historical Library in San Francisco. Other libraries that were used included those of the University of California at Los Angeles, Davis and Riverside; various branches of the Harvard University Library, specifically the Stanley Elkins Library, James Clay Frick Library, John F. Kennedy School of Government Library of Industrial Relations and the Houghton Archives. A note of thanks also goes to the San Francisco Public Library, the Fresno Public Library, the Riverside Public Library, the Los Angeles Public Library, California State University San Jose Library, the Santa Clara University Library and the California State Library in Sacramento.

Table of Contents

Acknowledgments   iii
Introduction   1
Background   6
The Economic Vise   15
The Chamber and the Waterfront   18
The Formation of the Law and Order Committee   25
The Radicals   36
Public Backing for the Committee   41
Charles Evans Hughes in San Francisco   54
The Trial of William McDevitt   65
The Committee vs. the Unions   81
"The End of the Trail"   96
Civic Reaction to the Committee   110
The Demise of the Committee   122
Overview   125
Appendix I: Letter, Rolph–Koster   129
Appendix II: The Committee of One Hundred   131
Appendix III: Delegates, September 19, 1917, Meeting   132
Appendix IV: Top Contributors to Committee   133
Appendix V: Resignations and Cancellations from Chamber of Commerce, 1915–1917   134
Chapter Notes   135
Bibliography   146
   Secondary Sources   146
   Newspapers and Periodicals   149
   Primary Sources   150
Index   153

Frederick J. Koster, ca. 1920

Introduction

On September 11, 1974, the *Los Angeles Times* quoted William B. Saxbe, then the Attorney General of the United States, speaking to the Cleveland Ohio Realtor's Association. Violent crime was spreading so fast Saxbe stated, that vigilantes might organize to take the law into their own hands; "In some parts of the country we already have seen the first faint inklings of such action."[1] In that same year one of the most lucrative Hollywood productions was *Deathwish*, the saga of a one-man committee of vigilance.

Committees of vigilance, law and order committees or vigilantes are not new to the American scene. As local conditions become strained citizens are prone to organize for the betterment of the community whether it is to lobby for a new sewage treatment plant or to demand an end to the skyrocketing crime rate. If these local conditions become intolerable the citizens will band into tight semi-official groups which may tightrope-walk the limits of the law. And if the conditions are truly catastrophic, the citizens will actually break the law — with or without the support of the law enforcement agencies.

Usually when one thinks of a committee of citizens banding together one conjures pictures of a growing frontier town with too many gunmen and too few honest women. In San Francisco, circa nineteenth century, this was exactly the case. But rather than just a few ruffians the city was plagued with roving bands of hoodlums — the word itself coined in San Francisco — who were not adverse to setting the city on fire or carrying out acts of depredation in broad daylight with scores of witnesses. Eventually this unchecked violence led to the formation of the first Committee of Vigilance in 1851. A second Committee of Vigilance followed within a decade. Though the committees faded into obscurity the vigilante spirit remained as a dormant instinct in San Francisco heritage.[2]

In 1916 San Francisco, as it had been in 1848, was the economic and cultural hub of the West Coast. The random lawlessness which had contributed to making it the "wickedest city in the world" had declined considerably as American entered the twentieth century. By the end of World War I the Barbary Coast — long a hangout for ruffians and hoodlums — had disappeared. But even with the passing

2 Committee of Vigilance

of the Barbary Coast a new scourge was on the horizon: unionism. The ensuing struggle between labor and management would prove to be as bitter and prolonged as the war with the Sydney Ducks.

In 1916 the San Francisco Chamber of Commerce was faced with a challenge. Traditionally a passive organization, the Chamber found itself in the midst of a labor-management uproar. Labor disputes had crippled the city. A runaway inflation had played havoc with the economy. Anarchists, Socialists and other "vermin" seemed to be everywhere. Then, on July 22, 1916, the violence seemed to culminate when a bomb went off during a Preparedness Day Parade. Ten persons were killed and more than forty others were injured. The bombing seemed to crystallize the frustrations of the city and a call for action was heard from city hall to the docks.

By coincidence a special committee of the Chamber of Commerce, known as the Law and Order Committee, had just been formed to look into the labor disputes and violence which had precipitated because of them. In the days of crisis after the July 22 bombing this new committee suddenly found itself riding the crest of a wave of popularity. It was the right organization in the right place at the right time.

What makes the Law and Order Committee so unusual is its historical lateness. Nineteen-sixteen was in an era of miracles of the scientific age: airplanes, telegraph, telephone and railroads had become commonplace. America was a world power though we did not know it yet. Law and order had been established. Courts were in session. Policemen patrolled the streets. America was becoming of age.

But not only was the Law and Order Committee historically late, it was also politically early. It would not be until 1919 that the nation would begin purging itself of the "misfits." America was for Americans. Haywoods, Goldmans, Socialists, Anarchists, IWWs and dissidents were suspect. The spectre of the Russian Revolution tended to heighten the hysteria of what historians have labeled "The Great Red Scare," which was actually no more than one of the many periodic outbursts of chauvinistic patriotism. The ensuing rush to judgment lumped all of the radical community together, including labor, under one label: UnAmerican. Many radicals paid for their beliefs by being exiled to foreign shores. Unions were considered suspect at best. But by the time the Great Red Scare had gained momentum the Law and Order Committee was no longer in existence.

Although there is a substantial amount of literature concerning the effects of a period of hysteria on the population at large, very little has been written of how an ambitious group of officials can harness phobic energy and direct it toward its own particular ends. This is the ultimate game of chess. The Law and Order Committee had an ulterior driving design for San Francisco: the city-wide open shop. The bombing gave the Committee the impetus to implement its program.

The Law and Order Committee was a Committee of Vigilance but rather than in the tradition of quick, extra-legal action, the Committee stressed a more sophisticated marshalling of all of the resources within the business community. The blood to be spilled would be the black ink of contracts and cabals. People were to die but the method of shoot-first-ask-questions-later had been subordinated to the use of political pressure and public manipulation. But the impact of the Committee is still being felt in the 1980's.

Within the Chamber of Commerce a small coterie of men spoke vigorously for the open shop. It was through their energies that the Law and Order Committee was formed. Eventually these two organizations lost any clear-cut boundaries and few were sure which was a subcommittee of the other. Functioning as the head of both the Chamber and the Committee was Frederick J. Koster. Although his announced aim was to rid San Francisco of the "radical element" which harassed civic enterprises, he was also vitally interested in establishing a city-wide open shop. In his mind these two goals were not mutually exclusive. His perception of the realities of the labor situation were faulty, however, and he led San Francisco into a confrontation it ill afforded.

Koster also broke the time honored tradition that the Chamber of Commerce would maintain a low profile. Once the campaign for the open shop began it was impossible for the Chamber to stay out of the limelight. Every attack upon the Law and Order Committee carried with it a barb for the Chamber of Commerce and its president, the "gentleman thug."[3] Koster chaired both the Law and Order Committee and the Chamber of Commerce and his reputation, as well as that of the Chamber of Commerce, was somewhat marred by the sleazy operations in which the Law and Order Committee engaged.

A quick *coup de grace* seemed inevitable for the Committee. Usually a Committee of Vigilance lasts only long enough to solve the most catastrophic problems and then fades into historical obscurity.

But in the eleventh hour the Preparedness Day Bombing pumped vitality into the Committee. In Mooney and Billings the Committee imagined the naked truth of labor and the closed shop. The Mooney–Billings affair became the focus around which labor and business stood face-to-face.

On one side was Labor. Union leadership was as disgruntled with Thomas Mooney and Warren Billings as was management; but a stand had to be taken and labor supported the two. For years to come Labor would try desperately to pry itself free from the insinuation that Mooney and Billings represented the closed shop.

Then there was the Law and Order Committee. The Committee had been quite adept at linking the Preparedness Day Bombing to the open shop campaign and the Committee's popularity rose in proportion to the hysteria generated by the outrage. But in its support of the Mooney–Billings trials the Committee found itself supporting a District Attorney who was not above railroading two innocent men to the gas chamber. In the end the stench of a frame-up would be woven inextricably into the history of the Law and Order Committee.[4]

A third group of individuals affected by the labor–management disputes in San Francisco were civic officials and city leaders who pressed for cool heads in the heat of confrontation. Leading this unofficial coterie was James R. Rolph, Jr., mayor of San Francisco. In consistent attempts to serve as a moderator Rolph refused to ally himself with either faction and his consistent cool, logical and rational outlook helped alleviate some of the tension. Another outspoken member of this group was Fremont Older, an old line Progressive and editor of the San Francisco *Bulletin*. Older had won a measure of notoriety for pressing for the conviction of one-time city boss Abraham Ruef and then, immediately after Ruef's conviction, pressing for Ruef's parole. Older would repeat this about-face in the Mooney–Billings case as well.[5]

The smallest yet most vocal group of antagonists in the drama were the radicals. The three standout figures were William McDevitt, Emma Goldman and Alexander Berkman. William McDevitt was an election commissioner for the City and County of San Francisco. He was also a Socialist, which did little to endear him to the Committee. Berkman and Goldman were both Anarchists, the former printing an Anarchist periodical, *The Blast*, in San Francisco, and the latter publishing *Mother Earth* in New York. Between the two journals the Mooney–Billings affair was kept alive in the conscience of the radical community with the heavy barrage of propaganda from both *The Blast* and *Mother Earth*. The unions looked to this support with dubious enthusiasm and the Committee saw the periodicals as evil incarnate. Along with other minor radicals, Berkman, Goldman and McDevitt acted as irritants to the already tense situation.

Although it may be said that the Mooney–Billings trials were a stimulus to the Law and Order Committee, the trial itself is of peripheral interest to this work. The trial and its shortcomings has been covered in two erudite and excellent books, Richard H. Frost's *The Mooney Case* and Curt Gentry's *Frame-Up: The Incredible Case of Tom Mooney and Warren Billings*. The present work tries to determine how the Chamber of Commerce was able to become so powerful, whether or not the Committee was truly a Committee of Vigilance and whether, as has been speculated, the Law and Order Committee was responsible for the defeat of Charles Evans Hughes in his bid for the presidency of the United States.

Background

The changing of the centuries was more than a symbolic changing of three digits for the United States. It was a moment to reflect on the greatness of the previous century and look forward to the promise of a new age. Although the nineteenth century mentality began to fade with many Americans, many of the problems of that century continued to linger. The vogue of Social Darwinism had not ebbed. Unrestricted immigration agitated the fledgling labor unions. *Laissez-faire* was not yet a nostalgic memory and imperialism, evil when applied to Britain's foreign adventures but resounding with respectability in the age of Theodore Roosevelt, was alive and well in the Caribbean and South Pacific.

Often the new was as threatening as the old. The Molly Maguires may have been left behind but the Industrial Workers of the World were just as dedicated. Marxism, Anarchism, Unionism and Progressivism — sometimes regarded with equal disdain — were the philosophies to be weathered. It was the age of Babbit's youth.

San Francisco entered the twentieth century as a child of the Gold Rush. Since the 1850's it had been the social and industrial focus of the West Coast primarily because the city fathers had been quick to capitalize on their proximity to the gold country. Every item the miners wore, toiled with or ate was brought in by ship. When the goods landed, miners literally rushed to buy shovels, nails and whiskey at any price. Bourbon sold for as high as $30 a quart. Eggs went for $50 a dozen and boots were as high as $100 a pair. Nails literally went for their weight in gold, $192 per pound.

While the skyrocketing inflation drained the miners San Francisco real estate was booming. Anyone with enough capital to open a saloon could make a killing. To help divide the miner from his poke with greater speed the city soon developed the Barbary Coast, actually no more than a somewhat disreputable section of town comprised of cheap dives and cribs, very cheap brothels, which established for San Francisco the somewhat dubious recognition as the "wickedest city on earth." Along with the trollops and rotgut were such eccentrics as Oofty-Goofty — now an ice cream parlor chain — and Emperor Norton — immortalized by the company he banned from his kingdom.

Closer uptown the macabre Mammy Pleasant opened her bordello of mystery on Octavia Street. Complete with Voodoo rituals Mammy both shocked and satiated the rich of San Francisco. Then she blackmailed them. Bordering on the fringes of respectability was the fiery Lola Montez who was greeted more out of the miners' passion for women in general than for any talent she might have possessed.

San Francisco had also produced a unique cultural heritage. Enrico Caruso and Jenny Lind performed in San Francisco. Jack London and Frank Norris claimed it as home. So did C.E. Boles — known in the Mother Lode as Black Bart the P-0-8. Robert Lewis Stevenson and Samuel Clemens both spent time in the city by the bay. And in the twenties, when the Law and Order Committee would be just another moldy memory, a president of the United States would die under mysterious circumstances at the St. Francis Hotel.

But with increasing wealth came increasing crime. In the late 1850's the rage and severity of crime was so staggering that uptown residents feared for their safety. Gangs of disreputable characters such as the Sydney Ducks were not above setting the entire city on fire and did so on several occasions. In an attempt to not only maintain their own safety but to try to bring a semblance of law and order to the streets of San Francisco, these uptown citizens formed a Committee of Vigilance and proceeded to take the law into their own hands and administer justice as they saw fit. Not only did the Committee frighten the miscreants into fleeing San Francisco but it also frightened the budding state government in Sacramento. On June 2, 1856, Governor J. Neely Johnson ordered General William Tecumseh Sherman to raise members of the militia and take the stronghold of the vigilantes — known as "Fort Gunnybags" because of the bulwark of sandbags which had been constructed about the building. On June 4 the Governor declared San Francisco to be in a state of insurrection. After a series of complicating circumstances the Committee of Vigilance decided to disband as an official organization. But the spirit of the Committee of Vigilance was not dead.

Neither the high crime rate nor the high prices kept people from coming to California. People poured into San Francisco by the hundreds and with them came the need for industry. With the demand for more products came the demand for more labor, skilled and unskilled. Thus cheap Chinese labor flooded in from the Orient to work on the railroads. Later the Japanese would follow.

With this sudden influx of cheap labor the demand for unionization, which had been as weak in San Francisco as elsewhere in the nation, began to find a receptive audience. The city's geographic position made it difficult to recruit nonunion labor in case of a massive city-wide strike. Depending on the support of all the unions in San Francisco it would be possible to bring the entire city to an economic standstill.

Coupled with this aggressive demand for unionization was the problem of the so-called coolie labor. Originally the Chinese had been imported to work on the railroads but by 1870 the railroad had been completed and the coolie labor had begun to compete with the white labor force. By the late 1870's Denis Kearney, a local demagogue, struck a tender nerve when he began his campaign against coolie labor. For more than five years Kearney and his "sandlot" associates terrorized the Chinese community. Eventually Kearney and the Workingmen's Party, a party of his creation, collapsed. But the failure of the Workingmen's Party was based not on the inability of the Party to attract members but because its vitality was too closely linked with that of its founder. Once Kearney lost his credibility, so did the Workingmen's Party. Though the Party died the impetus toward the unionization was only momentarily stalled and a valuable lesson had been learned; it would be essential to keep the unions as an independent entity and away from the influence of any one person.

San Francisco broke into the twentieth century in tumultuous fashion. The spring of 1901 brought a massive strike, a harbinger of events to come. Several thousand metal workers demanding a closed or union shop began the strike and other unions began sympathy strikes. The business community, in fear that the strikes would mean an end to the open shop in San Francisco, felt compelled to form an association of their own. This association, known as the Employers' Alliance, temporarily unified the business community into a single, monolithic organization which could negotiate with the unions.

The Employers' Alliance also used a new weapon in their arsenal: a product boycott. In addition to the usual public statements deploring the strikes, the Alliance also pressured the business community not to buy or deal with products made in a closed shop. The product boycott brought a temporary lull in the strike as the unions were ill equiped to face the united front of the employers. But the strike was far from over.

Several weeks later the restaurant workers, culinary unions

and several other unions walked off their jobs. Having learned from the metal workers strike how effective the boycott had been for the Employers' Alliance, the unions began a boycott of their own. Other unions were urged to join in the boycott. But the most effective ingredient in the boycott was the joining of the longshoremen and the powerful drayage or inner-city transport companies to the ranks of the strikers. (Because of San Francisco's dependence on the dock workers, a strike on the waterfront would paralyze the city.) By July 30, 1901, all transportation within the city had come to a halt and violence plagued the streets of San Francisco.

It appeared that no agreement could be reached between the strikers and the employers. What was needed was a catalyst; this was provided in the form of Governor Henry T. Gage. Gage flatly stated that unless a settlement was reached in ten days he would declare a state of emergency and order the National Guard into San Francisco to restore law and order. The thought of National Guardsmen patrolling San Francisco did not sit well with either side and a settlement was quickly reached. But neither side was satisfied with the new contracts and the labor situation remained strained and animosity between the unions and management would remain for years.

Several weeks later city elections were held. It seemed the ideal opportunity for the labor unions to consolidate their power, if not on the streets then definitely in the city government. Union members, believing that the city government was manipulated by the business interests and the Employers' Alliance, organized a political party to counteract the supposed political machine of the employers. Unifying their energy behind a single ticket the unions formed the Union Labor Party. For mayor they nominated an orchestra leader and violin player, Eugene F. Schmitz. His surprising victory marked the Union Labor Party as a major power in San Francisco and was acknowledged as a harbinger for labor throughout the United States.

It was not long, however, before it became apparent that Eugene Schmitz was not the person who held the power. Schmitz may have been the mayor but the true power lay with an able attorney by the name of Abraham Ruef. Ruef controlled the Union Labor Party and the city administration as though they were his own private kingdom.

Ruef had started college as an idealist — his senior thesis was entitled *Purity in Politics* — but after a cold, hard look at the political realities of the time he adapted himself in the style of a Machiavellian.

He saw in the Union Labor Party an excellent opportunity for a young and ambitious lawyer. He began in the Union Labor Party as a grassroots worker but his political expertise and legal knowledge soon elevated him rapidly to the higher echelons of the party. Gradually he worked himself into the position where his decisions were so fundamental to the operation of the city government that he was known as "Boss" Ruef. Working behind the scenes, where he preferred to be, his expert advice had been a significant factor in the election of Schmitz and he garnered the spoils of a union leader in the mayorship.

The politics of the first four years of the Schmitz administration were turbulent. The other city officials, neither promanagement nor prounion, were reluctant to side with the new union administration, thus making it difficult for Schmitz to replace union men in the city administration with any speed. It took until 1905, two city elections later, before the Schmitz-Ruef machine was firmly entrenched in city hall. Then came the payola.

Installing himself as the vital link between city hall and the business community Ruef let it be known throughout the larger businesses in San Francisco that with Ruef as their attorney they could not fail to win approval for their contracts with the city. All franchises from small fruitcar licenses to multimillion dollar railroad contracts were channeled through Ruef's office. Though his fees were exorbitant his services were guaranteed.

At first there was little public reaction to the graft within the Schmitz administration. Those that did not know of the corruption tended to put any insinuation of graft down as rumor. Those who were aware of the corruption felt that it was what was to be expected of twentieth century business and government. But there were enough citizens who were dissatisfied with the corruption to start an anticorruption campaign, albeit a low key one. Rumor ran through the city administration that some action was impending but before any move could be initiated disaster struck.

On the morning of April 18, 1906, San Franciscans were suddenly shaken awake by a tremor that shook the entire state. Buildings toppled covering streets, trolleys and people. Water mains broke beneath the twisting earth. Drunken mobs, under the impression that Judgment Day had finally arrived, looted the city with impunity. Then the fires started.

The quake did little damage in comparison to the fires which followed in its wake. Overturned stoves and broken lanterns soon set several major blazes which ran unchecked throughout the city. Unfortunately many of the tenements in San Francisco were not much better than tinderboxes and the fires swept through them at a speed which at times was faster than a horse could run. The water system, designed to save San Francisco from just such conflagrations, had been ruptured and the city lay helpless.

To augment the city's fire department the United States Navy had to be called in to fight the fire and restore law and order. After three days of dynamiting buildings in the fires' paths and impressing able-bodied men into service the fire finally died out. But San Francisco was left a blackened core. More than 514 blocks of the central city had been burned. More than 28,000 buildings were totally destroyed. Losses were conservatively estimated at around 500 million dollars and more than 450 persons perished in the disaster.

When the smoke cleared San Francisco began to pull itself together again. Water and food were lacking. Sanitation was so bad that a typhus epidemic was expected. Looting was still widespread. Within 24 hours, however, San Francisco was once again a tent city reminiscent of its Gold Rush heritage. The Red Cross began drafting people into its ranks and the cleanup began. Like the proverbial phoenix, San Francisco rose from its own ashes.

Despite the fact that San Francisco had been ushered into a new era by the earthquake and fire, the problems of corruption in the city administration remained unsolved. The anti-Schmitz feeling that had begun to grow before the quake suddenly rekindled. Since San Francisco had lost most of its public transportation in the fire there was a real need for new as well as additional lines. In the interest of the United Railroads, owned by Patrick Calhoun, Ruef pressed city hall for a franchise. It was alleged that Ruef's fee was $200,000. The immediate, gruesome conclusion by many was that Ruef was making a profit at the expense of the charred and burnt bodies of the holocaust. The outrage was intense.

A meeting was called to organize a movement to throw Schmitz and his cohorts out of office. The leaders of this purge movement were the former mayor of San Francisco, James D. Phelan; the Progressive editor of the San Francisco *Bulletin*, Fremont Older; and a wealthy businessman, Rudolph Spreckles. (A decade later Older and Spreckles would once again be allied during the Billings affair.) Older went to Washington, D.C., and through the aid of Theodore Roosevelt was able to obtain the services of Francis J. Heney. Heney, known for his intensive investigations and tough prosecution in cases of corruption, began his sleuthing in what culminated in the "Graft Trials."

But Ruef was not to be defeated without a fight. When the district attorney of San Francisco, William J. Langdon, announced his intention to aid in the prosecution of Ruef, Ruef showed his genius for *finesse*. Mayor Schmitz was conveniently away on vacation and James L. Gallager, chairman of the Board of Supervisors, acting as mayor fired Langdon and appointed Ruef as the district attorney. Langdon, however, refused to leave his post. Ruef ordered him out of the office and Langdon went to court. After several hearings Langdon's position was upheld. This was the beginning of the end for Ruef as little stood in the way of a complete investigation and the inevitable tumble of "Boss" Ruef from power.

Ruef's trial was dramatic and included little justice but much that showed the trial to be a travesty. Jurors were bribed, documents were stolen, a witness' house was bombed, Fremont Older was "kidnapped" and Heney was gunned down *in open court*. A young San Francisco attorney by the name of Hiram Johnson was chosen to take Heney's place. In the end only Ruef went to prison.

Despite Ruef's conviction there remained the clear, yet ugly message that political influence and favors could be bought and that the dangers were all borne by the bribe-taker—not the bribe-giver. Ruef was in jail yet William F. Herrin and Patrick Calhoun, the alleged bribe-givers, remained free. This fact appalled Fremont Older. All the campaign against corruption had done was remove the figurehead of the graft. Feeling that a great injustice had been done to Ruef, Older did an about-face and began pressing for Ruef's parole with as much vigor as he had pressed for Ruef's trial. Older's apostasy was hard for many to understand.

In spite of the damage done to the union cause by the Schmitz–Ruef machine the unions had gained in strength. The coming-of-age of the unions was accelerated by the sudden demand for construction after the earthquake and fire. Especially powerful in San Francisco was the Building Trades Council. Within three years the Building Trades Council had rebuilt more than 70% of the gutted city and carried enough political clout to elect one of their members, P.H. "Pinhead" McCarthy, to the mayorship. (In the same 1909 election the Union Labor Party supported Charles M. Fickert* for the district

---

*Fickert was a football hero from the same Stanford team on which Herbert Hoover was waterboy.

attorneyship. Within a decade the unions would press for his dismissal because of his questionable, if not illegal, handling of the Mooney–Billings Case.)

But the McCarthy victory was short-lived. In 1911 James R. "Sunny" Rolph was elected mayor. The candidate running against him on the Socialist Ticket—and pulling a strong third—was William McDevitt, a man who would haunt the history of legal annals. (Also on the Socialist ticket was a young Thomas J. Mooney running for sheriff.)

Rolph proved to be far more acceptable to the voters of San Francisco than representatives of unions. Being a businessman, the business community felt secure with him in city hall. And though he was not a union man in a town where unions were exceptionally strong, his impartiality allowed him to remain mayor for twenty years.

During the twenty years of Rolph's administration, San Francisco began to expand outward from the core that had been rebuilt after the earthquake and fire. Two pet projects of the Rolph Administration were a municipally owned and operated streetcar system—a dream which did not thrill the United Railroads—and the construction of an aqueduct to bring water to San Francisco from the Sierra Nevadas. The former, known as MUNI, was completed in 1917 at a cost of 4.5 million dollars but the latter was still a dream when Rolph left San Francisco to become Governor of California.

Rolph also had the city hall rebuilt and created the Civic Center Plaza, which is still in existence today. In spite of the fact that many doubted that San Francisco would ever recover from the earthquake and fire, the city was sufficiently rebuilt by 1915 to host the Panama–Pacific Exposition. This was considered by the citizens of San Francisco to be the beginning of a new age in American history—not to mention the beginning of commercial trade which was expected to increase substantially because of the canal.

But the labor problems which had plagued San Francisco since the turn of the century had not disappeared. Business, unlike labor, was reluctant to organize and continually found itself hopelessly fragmented. The Employers' Alliance of 1901 had been effective for a year. In 1912 a group was formed named the Citizen's Alliance but it failed to shake off the lethargy which seemed to grip the business community. Finally, in 1914, a small group of businessmen formed an organization known as the Merchants and Manufacturers Association of San Francisco which began making headway.

As its greatest hope lay in consolidation of power, the Merchants and Manufacturers Association attempted to gain the support of the drayage companies in hopes of preventing the unions from exercising this exclusive control as they had done so effectively in 1901. But the drayage companies had been so financially devastated by the strike of 1901 that they were not about to rush into any costly labor dispute. They would, however, consider joining the Merchants and Manufacturers Association if that organization would agree to put up a large sum of money as security against any strike-incurred losses. The price proved to be prohibitive.[1]

But even if the alliance had been consummated, historians feel that any labor–business confrontation was not in the offing for 1915. The Panama–Pacific Exposition, that great honor San Francisco had garnered, kept the business and labor communities from any serious confrontation. It was the tacit understanding in both camps that nothing must be done to mar the image of San Francisco at the Exposition. But the storm clouds were brewing. On January 1, 1915, the *Labor Clarion*, a Bay Area labor publication, advised the unions to "husband" their resources during 1915.[2] The unions had already begun to brace for the impending struggle a year and a half before it actually broke out!

Although labor was expecting a confrontation, the business community was still badly divided. No previous organization had ever formed a viable nucleus around which the other businesses could gather. The only ingredient that many businesses had in common, especially the larger firms, was membership in the San Francisco Chamber of Commerce. Although the San Francisco Chamber of Commerce had had a vested interest in many of the defunct business alliances, the Chamber had preferred to play a spectator role rather than involve itself as an active participant in any labor–management dispute. In 1916 it appeared that this policy would not change. Short of actual war the Chamber of Commerce would again avoid any direct involvement in the labor–management confrontations.

The Economic Vise

The year 1916 seemed tailor-made for labor–management confrontation. Hysteria over the United States' possible involvement in World War I combined with the spreading antiradical sentiment seemed to put the nation on edge. The economic picture added a bleak backdrop to the deteriorating labor peace.

During the previous few years there had been a gradual yet steadily rising rate of inflation which had been gnawing perceptibly away at the earnings of the workers. It was the hope of the unions that the war in Europe would stimulate a demand for American products and thus bring the inflationary period to a close. America, at least until 1918, looked upon itself more as a supplier than as an active ally to any power in Europe.

To the unions the panacea to the economic ills of San Francisco was increased demand of San Francisco goods and services. This would cause employment to rise to meet the production quotas and an increase in wages would be expected to follow shortly thereafter. Additionally, San Francisco firms were hopeful that the Federal government would contract heavily in San Francisco for steel and labor to build additional harbor facilities for an American Pacific Fleet as its unique harbor and proximity to the Panama Canal made it more commercially, as well as defensively, attractive than many other West Coast ports. The resulting contracts would in turn stimulate indigenous industries. This was an enviable dream.

In reality, however, the increased demand led to more vociferous demands by unions for increased wages. Workmen were not content in 1916 to accept wages which had been at mere subsistence levels in 1910. But the unions found themselves in a pinch. The labor market had grown by almost 70 percent since the turn of the century and the strain on the unions was immense. They were forced to incorporate many new members or face the possibility of roving bands of scabs available to business during a strike. When, in the past, management might have had to have sent as far away as Chicago for nonunion labor, now there was a supply within the city limits. And, as the unions incorporated more members and demanded higher wages, inflation continued to rise.

Despite previous efforts by the San Francisco business community to curtail the power of the unions, the labor unions had remained strong. In 1901 the concerted efforts of the business community had been mustered to force the issue of the open shop and the only result had been a stalemate. By 1916 antiunion sentiment was still present in the city but by no means greater than it had been fifteen years earlier. Over the years the behind-the-scenes efforts by the business community to check the power of the unions had flowered, and died, and the unions continued to remain powerful both economically and politically.

Indeed, many businesses gave support to the labor movement, if only token support. Those most reluctant to involve themselves in a labor war were the smaller, local businesses which depended almost entirely on the unions for workers and supplies. Most of the smaller enterprises, restaurants, minor shipping firms and the crucial intercity transport firms were directly dependent on the unions. To them labor peace was a far better bargain than a protracted labor war.

The businessmen primarily interested in securing the open shop, a shop in which union membership was not a condition of employment, were the larger industries that did not depend directly on organized labor. A great majority of these were members of the San Francisco Chamber of Commerce and represented some of the most prestigious firms in San Francisco. Among these were the Santa Fe and Southern Pacific Railroads, Bank of California, Standard Oil of California, Emporium, Shell Oil Company, Wells Fargo Bank, Bank of America, Dollar Steamship Line and the San Francisco Commercial Club. Since these businesses controlled a substantial pool of capital resources they had the finances to weather a long and costly battle with the unions. This immediately set them apart from the smaller businesses.

The union community in San Francisco was prodigious. The majority of organized labor was represented by several large unions, among them the San Francisco Building Trades Council,* International Longshoremen's Union, San Francisco Culinary Union, San Francisco Labor Council and Waterfront Workers Federation. Collectively these organizations represented over 185 different, smaller unions and had a membership that exceeded 80,000. It was the largest and most powerful conglomerate on the West Coast.[1]

While grievances over shop conditions constituted a major issue,

---

The San Francisco Building Trades Council had declined in power following the earthquake and fire of 1906.

inflation was the catalyst. Between 1906 and 1916 the average wage of a working man in San Francisco rose 16 percent while in the same period the price of food advanced 39 percent. The cost of food in San Francisco was charted in an independent survey presented to the Commonwealth Club of California by Ira B. Cross of the University of California. Using as a base the total price of twenty foods— including flour, meat, potatoes, beans and fish—Dr. Cross established a base cost in March 1907 of $13.71. By December of 1915 this price had risen to $16.35; in December of 1916 it was $19.77 and at the end of the survey in December, 1917, the price of the foods was listed as $26.23. There had been a rise of over 59 percent in the twelve months of 1917 alone. Coupled with this were a corresponding 84 percent increase in the cost of food overall, a 115 percent increase in the cost of clothing and a 125 percent increase in the cost of furniture. It has been estimated that the top of this rising inflation was not reached until July of 1920 at a high which would not be equaled again until 1947.[2]

Within this tight economic vise the unions began demanding higher wages. By 1916 the number of strikes had grown and the average duration of the strikes increased and the strikers became more prone to violence. Concessions, if and when they were granted, were given only grudgingly and the actual union gains were small.[3]

The citizens of San Francisco, those not directly involved with either labor or management, saw the city on the threshold of another era of protracted lawlessness. As inflation prompted strikes, and strikes prompted backlash, San Franciscans braced themselves for a full-fledged labor war. All that was needed was a spark to set off the powder keg. That spark was not long in coming.

The Chamber
and the Waterfront

San Francisco's first major strike in 1916 began on June 1. In conjunction with the West Coast branch of the International Longshoremen's Association (ILA), the San Francisco ILA members walked off their jobs. On the same day the Bay and River Steamboatmen's Union struck the Bay Area. Shipping on the West Coast was virtually paralyzed, with more than 10,000 ILA members on strike, 4,000 of them in San Francisco alone.

This was the first unified walkout on the West Coast. The primary strategy was to force a wage settlement with the employers. The ILA demands for an increase to 55 cents an hour for straight time and $1 an hour for overtime after nine hours were more than the employers were willing to pay. The Bay and River Steamboatmen's Union were asking for a $5 a month salary increase.[1]

These strikes galled the San Francisco Waterfront Employers Union (WEU), an organization of waterfront businessmen. After nearly two years of extended negotiation, the WEU and the ILA had agreed in December of 1915 that no strike would be called before a 60-day cooling-off period had elapsed. Section 18 of their agreement read as follows:

> This agreement to remain in full force and effect from December 31, 1915, and to continue in effect thereafter until either party shall give notice to the other party in writing of their desire to have same changed. Such notice shall be given at least sixty days prior to said change going into effect.[2]

The agreement was validated by some of the most powerful figures in the business and labor communities. Signing for the ILA was John Kean, president of the Riggers and Stevedores Union Local 38. Management was represented by R.P. Schwerin and R.C. Thackara, president and secretary of the Waterfront Employers Union respectively. The agreement was witnessed by Rowland B. Mahany, commissioner of conciliation for the United States Department of Labor.[3]

The contract was signed on December 23, 1915. On May 9, 1916, the ILA announced that a strike would commence on June 1. This left only a 22-day waiting-period between the announcement of the strike and the commencement date. It appeared that the unions were intent on violating the contract.

If the Waterfront Employers Union was distraught, the United States Department of Labor was outraged. After putting the prestige of its office on the line to witness the contract it was not pleased to see that contract junked. This would be considered a betrayal. On June 3, a telegram from William B. Wilson, United States Secretary of Labor, was sent to ILA Local 38 in San Francisco urging the strikers to return to work. Wilson stated that the violation of the contract would do irreparable damage to the prospects of similar labor negotiations in the future and would devastate the Department of Labor's credibility in San Francisco. In the telegram he stated:

> The statement that you are not proposing to change the agreement deceives no one. You cannot conceal such an agreement without changing it for something else.... No union can long exert an influence for good which deliberately violates its contract for temporary gain where the honor and integrity of any union can be justly assailed on the grounds of bad faith.[4]

Wilson assigned another Federal mediator to meet with the ILA and WEU and finally, on June 9, a partial settlement was reached. Wages would be raised to the level demanded by the unions but ongoing negotiations concerning permanent wages could reduce this temporary gain.[5]

For the San Francisco ILA the strike had been a disastrous undertaking. On one hand, since San Francisco was the largest employer of longshoremen on the West Coast, any strike by ILA which did not include San Francisco could not be successful. But on the other hand the San Francisco ILA was tied to a new contract. Thus the ILA had been forced to choose between honor to a contract or commitment to the national union. It had chosen the latter.

But the strike had become a fiasco. There was little hope of receiving the support of local unions in San Francisco for no other reason than that the ILA had flagrantly violated the terms of its own contract. This violation was obvious to the other unions as well as to both management and the public at large.

To make matters worse, when the San Francisco ILA members

returned to work they had broken the solidarity of the West Coast ILA and weakened the impact of a coast-wide strike. Their abrupt withdrawal after only eight days into a major walkout threatened to break the entire West Coast strike. But the greatest tragedy was that the San Francisco ILA had made no appreciable gains.

At best, the settlement was a partial solution to the San Francisco waterfront turbulence. In spite of the facts that the riggers and stevedores were back at work, the waterfront lumberyard workers were unaffected by the new contract. Rather than submit to the demands of the unions, the lumberyard management organized the Retail Lumber Dealers' Association to fight the ILA.[6]

The situation in the lumberyards worsened when the Waterfront Employers Union announced that it would begin to import strikebreakers to work in the lumberyards. Violence broke out around the lumberyards and soon became so intense that the WEU was forced to place armed guards in the vicinity to protect the strikebreakers. The situation became critical on June 18 when a union striker was shot and killed by an armed guard.

The ILA was quick to charge the WEU with complicity to murder. Furthermore, the ILA announced that unless all armed guards left the docks immediately it would return to strike conditions. The WEU refused and on June 22, thirteen days after it had agreed to a new contract, ILA members walked off their jobs once again. In those two weeks, four persons had been beaten and one killed on the San Francisco waterfront.[7]

Negotiations for the settlement of the second waterfront strike began on July 1. The WEU offered the ILA no specific wage increases this time but insisted that the ILA return to work for the wages of June 1 while negotiations continued. A final settlement date of August 1 was guaranteed for all wage matters. No provision was made for the removal of either the armed guards or the nonunion labor from the lumberyards. Reluctantly the ILA voted to accept this new contract on July 17.[8]

The second ILA strike settlement did not endear the WEU to the ILA. Both strikes had been fiascos. The first strike was inexcusable because of the outrageous violation of the December, 1915, contract with the WEU. The second strike was an even grosser violation of the December 1915 contract. Neither strike had achieved any appreciable gains and in many quarters of San Francisco it was the opinion of labor and management alike that the San Francisco ILA did not know what it was doing.

The Chamber and the Waterfront 21

By July 17 an ossifying effect had begun to take hold of the business community. Management, jolted by the ILA violations, began pressing for an organization to speak on their behalf. It was their feeling that a unified voice of business must be heard above the hubbub of labor and government in regard to San Francisco labor disputes. The logical focus of this organization would be the San Francisco Chamber of Commerce.

As the attention of the business community began to focus on the Chamber of Commerce, influential members of that body began to realize that this would be an opportune moment to harness the agitated business community to a city-wide open shop campaign — the pet scheme that had been brewing in management circles since the stalemate of 1901.

The contemporary philosophy which seemed to go hand-in-hand with the open shop was that of Social Darwinism. Strongly insinuated with the tenets of the theory was the denunciation of collective bargaining as "unnatural." Unions would not only organize labor but eventually they would disrupt the "natural" balance between labor and management. Though unions were a phenomenon of long standing in San Francisco this did not make them immune from the persistent rumor that they were responsible for the galloping inflation.

The business community felt that the unions were responsible for the high cost of living in San Francisco. Wage demands were the root evil which accelerated inflation. Yet in a single stroke the open shop would eliminate both the inflation and the unions. As a fringe benefit the city-wide open shop would force the "outside agitators" to go elsewhere to organize. With this philosophy in vogue it was not hard to imagine that the Chamber of Commerce was a hotbed of antiunion sentiment and the city-wide open shop was more of a crusade than a campaign.

The shift of the Chamber of Commerce from a dormant organization to an aggressive one began in May, 1916 when the Chamber elected its new officers:

Frederick J. Koster	President
Seward B. McNear	First Vice President
Robert Newton Lynch	Second Vice President
George C. Boardman	Third Vice President
James J. Fogan	Treasurer
L.M. King	Secretary[9]

These men comprised a fresh and energetic administration which began immediately to consider what action might be taken in the wake of the waterfront situation. Up to this time the Chamber had always maintained a strict, self-imposed policy of nonintervention in labor disputes but on June 20 a special meeting was called to discuss the waterfront disturbances. In an effort to help mediate a settlement that would include the lumberyards as well as the Bay and River Steamboatmen's Union, the Chamber formed a committee of three to consider what action was "to be taken in regard to the waterfront situation." This special committee formulated a resolution which was introduced to the entire Chamber in the following form:

> Therefore the Chamber of Commerce pledges its entire organization and the resources it represents to the maintenance of those principles [law and order along the waterfront] and will oppose any attempt on the part of any interest, business or organization which tries to throttle the commercial freedom of San Francisco.[10]

This cautiously worded resolution marked the beginning of the rejection of the traditional low profile which the Chamber had maintained for years. It was also a potential bomb if the unions chose to interpret it as a call to arms. The resolution was well received at the June 22 meeting of the Chamber.

Tactically the Chamber of Commerce was attempting to bluff the unions because at that time it did not have the support of the membership at large to force the unions to a settlement. Open shop was a pipe dream at best and any declaration by the Chamber of Commerce was regarded by the unions as just so much hot air. In its June 22 issue, the *Labor Clarion* did report the Chamber's resolution and stated it constituted a "declaration of war."[11] However, the unions did not take the Chamber of Commerce seriously.

But the Chamber's resolution did awe many of the smaller businesses who were frightened of what they interpreted as the preliminary push for the open shop. These establishments were more inclined to give in to the demands of the unions rather than risk a lengthy, costly strike. While existing economic conditions were not the best in San Francisco history they were considerably better than what could be expected if the Chamber of Commerce pressed for a city-wide open shop. If the conflict in Europe continued to create a demand for San Francisco goods and services the inflation might be stopped but statements such as the one issued by the Chamber would only serve to aggravate the already tense situation.

Less than a week after it had gone on record for law and order the Chamber began to press behind the scenes for the open shop. But the most important component of any such campaign would be the united support of its membership and the business community. The logical organization to woo was the Waterfront Employer's Union.

But the WEU was not interested in becoming involved in such a campaign. An open shop would first mean a lockout. Financial aid to force a lockout was difficult to find and assistance by the Chamber of Commerce could be considered transitory at best. Even if the financial aid could be found there would be the need for an adequate amount of manpower to maintain the waterfront. Without money and manpower the lockout would be ineffective.

Wishing to stay clear of the Chamber of Commerce the WEU announced on June 26 that it wished no part of the open shop campaign. It even offered to increase hourly wages to 55 cents straight time and 82.5 cents for overtime in addition to a guarantee to remove the strikebreakers upon final settlement of the contract. This left the Chamber of Commerce in a rather ticklish situation. If the Chamber wanted to become involved on the waterfront its efforts would lack legitimacy without the support of the WEU. Consequently the Chamber requested a meeting with the WEU and a nebulous agreement — never made public — was reached.[12] The successful wooing of the WEU was the first step in the Chamber's path to the open shop.

Complicating the agreement, however, was the fact that the WEU was still in negotiations with the Federal mediator. Oddly enough as late as July 17 the WEU was making concessions to the longshoremen and it was quite apparent to many observers that the support of the Chamber by the WEU was lukewarm. As time would tell, the association of the WEU and the Chamber was destined to become so close that the WEU was forced to follow wherever the Chamber led.

Into late June and early July the situation along the waterfront did not improve. The drayage companies were not on strike but they were required to obtain a special permit before they were allowed to get through the picket lines. The permits were issued by the Riggers' and Stevedores' Union and were given only to those businesses friendly to the cause of labor. Drayage workers without a permit friendly to the cause of labor. Drayage workers without a permit were turned away or sometimes beaten. With the increasing violence the tolerance of the waterfront merchants began to erode. One businessman, John Renner of the International Flour Company, addressed a bitter letter to Mayor James R. Rolph, Jr., condemning the Chamber for its strong advocacy to the open shop—which put the unions into a belligerent uproar—and at the same time its lack of action to accomplish this end:

> Such meetings as have been held by the Chamber of Commerce amount to nothing, as they simply declare for an open shop, but do nothing, to enforce this and San Francisco remains today a more closed shop than it ever was, for the simple reason that merchants are scared to death to conduct their business and it is outrageous that such conditions exist in a supposedly free society.[13]

Rolph, a member of the Chamber of Commerce but not a proponent of its program, returned a diplomatic letter to Renner assuring him that the "Police Department of San Francisco is able to maintain law and order in the community at all times.[14] This probably did little to soothe the rage of Renner and his compatriots.

By July 4 there had been 17 recorded beatings and one death reported along the waterfront. On July 5 six nonunion men were hospitalized when widespread violence rocked the docks. The Chamber, represented by Frederick J. Koster, demanded that the mayor immediately place an additional 500 police officers on the docks to restore law and order. Rolph refused, declaring that he would not sanction any "extra-legal" army in San Francisco, but did order the police to search all strikebreakers for concealed weapons.[15]

The mayor's rejection of the Chamber's demand forced it to make a choice. It was either to be an all-out confrontation or an ignominious retreat back to its policy of nonintervention. The Chamber had tried to bluff the unions and had failed. The Chamber had tried to use its influence as a wedge and force the mayor to support its position and that too had failed. To surrender was unthinkable. Not only would such a policy destroy the credibility of the Chamber of Commerce but it would undoubtedly mark the beginning of a rapid union takeover in San Francisco. The confrontation over open shop was inexorable and the Chamber girded its loins for the Armaggedon.

The Formation of the Law and Order Committee

> *The Law and Order program is founded in a spirit of love for our city, a recognition of the wonderful opportunity of her people, and a belief in her great destiny. The Law and Order program insists upon a respect for the Constitution of the United States, a respect so deep that it may not with impunity be assailed and it insists upon respect for the American flag and all it represents of the spirit of human liberty.* — Law and Order Committee Program, 1916.[1]

On July 10 Frederick J. Koster used his prerogative as president of the Chamber of Commerce to call a special meeting. The moment was propitious to attract a large number of members. Since the meeting on June 22 when the Chamber had gone on record supporting law and order on the waterfront, more than 39 beatings had occurred along the waterfront. The Bay and River Steamboat Owner's Association had not settled with its striking union, the auto mechanics were on strike, the structural steel workers had walked off their jobs that morning and the city's culinary workers had threatened a city-wide shutdown. It was the Chamber's strategy to harness the simmering discontent of the business community to press for the city-wide open shop.

For several days widespread publicity and circulars announced the meetings. From the circulars, especially those sent from the Chamber of Commerce, it appeared that the city was under siege. The circulars read:

> An intolerable situation exists on the waterfront. Intimidation prevents merchants from receiving or delivering goods from or to certain docks.... Law and Order must be maintained in San Francisco. YOU ARE URGED TO BE AT THIS MEETING WITHOUT FAIL. If you have the interest of San Francisco at heart you will be there! This is a matter of urgent duty and should cancel any other business engagements.[2]

On the afternoon of July 10 more than 2000 irate businessmen gathered to demand action. The meeting was chaired by Koster and included a list of guest speakers which boasted some of the most influential men in the San Francisco business community: Frank B. Anderson, president of the Bank of California; Philip S. Teller, president of the San Francisco Commercial Club; William Sproule, president of the Southern Pacific Railroad; R.I. Bentley of the California Fruit Canners Association and Robert Dollar of the Dollar Steamship Line.[3]

Of all the speakers Dollar was the most notorious in the eyes of labor. In the past Dollar had been the "champion of coolie labor," a position which had infuriated the unions not so much from a racial as economic point of view since the Chinese were willing to work for less than a union member could accept. As a result, in a tight labor market the Chinese would be working while the union member starved. Dollar added to his already sordid reputation by summing up at the mass meeting with the statement that the best way to settle the waterfront disturbance was to "send several ambulance loads of strikers to the hospitals."[4]

In the keynote address Koster outlined the union conflict along the waterfront and set forth the position of the Chamber of Commerce:

> This is a meeting of the members of the Chamber of Commerce of the merchants, manufacturers and businessmen of San Francisco and their associates.... It is called for the purpose of considering the intolerable conditions prevailing upon the waterfront and the disease permeating this community, of which the waterfront situation is at present the most outstanding manifestation, to the end that positive and determined action may be taken toward the permanent eradication, and of giving every element of the community full notice of that determination.[5]

Koster made it quite clear that the Chamber viewed all radical activity in San Francisco to be an integral part of the demand for unionization and the closed shop. He tied this thread effectively by reviewing the breaking of the December contract by the Riggers and Stevedores Union Local 38 and listed the incidents of violence and

Opposite: The July 10 Chamber of Commerce mass meeting of businessmen to form the Law and Order Committee.

what action had been taken in each case. Speaking of labor unions he tried to straddle the issue with generality. "The Chamber is not out to destroy labor unions," he stated "nor will it undertake anything of that character."[6] The Chamber, he affirmed, was primarily interested in ending the "rule of the associated agitators, criminals and criminal apologists" and taking aggressive action in the "fight for the God-given right of every individual to work."[7]

Koster reaffirmed the June 22 stand of the Chamber of Commerce and announced the formation of a special Law and Order Committee which would operate under a three-fold program: the maintenance of law and order, the right of business to employ either union or nonunion labor, and the scrupulous maintenance of contracts.[8]

Koster named himself chairman of the Law and Order Committee. The other members were C.R. Johnson of the Union Lumberyard; George M. Rolph (the mayor's brother), of the California and Hawaiian Sugar Refining Company; C.F. Michaels of Langly & Michaels Wholesale Drugs, and Wallace M. Alexander of Alexander and Baldwin, Ltd., Shipping and Commission Merchants. Hugh M. Webster was named as confidential secretary and the law firm of Metson, Drew and McKenzie was named as special counsel.[9]

The law firm was a rather ironic choice for the Law and Order Committee. The head of the firm, William "Billy" Metson, had already established himself in the annals of the West as a vigilante. Known as "Hell Fire Bill from Gold Hill" and "Two Gun Billy," Metson had gained a reputation in Alaska as the law "North of 53." For years he carried two guns from former associates, "Pinoche" Kelley and Pat Reedy, both of whom had been "early Nevada and California mining men, both of whom had been fast on the draw on several occasions." His early life had been spiced with an alleged love affair with "The Great Emma Nevada" who was known by some as "the world's greatest coloratura singer." Billy Metson's life was so colorful that it was used as a model for the character Billy Wheaton in Rex E. Beach's *The Spoilers*.[10] It was odd that such a man would be chosen to represent the Law and Order Committee.

With overwhelming approval of the Chamber the Law and Order Committee was established. During the next three years the Chamber would gradually slip into the background as its more aggressive offspring took the limelight. All matters relating to labor were funneled through the Law and Order Committee and though this streamlined the process of having labor difficulties reach the membership of the Chamber it also excluded rank and file members from any decision-making role. As time wore on, all decisions over the labor situation would be made by the Committee and the terms "Chamber of Commerce," "Law and Order Committee" and "Frederick J. Koster" became synonymous.

Since Koster was president of the Chamber of Commerce as well as the Law and Order Committee he naturally drew whatever criticism was launched at either organization. For the labor community in San Francisco he rapidly became the symbol of the open shop. "Kaiser Koster," "The Gentleman Thug" and "Kosterization" became common phrases from the lips of union men in San Francisco.[11]

Perhaps this characterization was inaccurate since Koster was somewhat of an anomaly for the position he held. As president of the California Barrel Company he did not attempt to institute the open shop but generously granted his employees wage increases and instituted the eight-hour day of his own volition. At the height of the campaign for a city-wide open shop — of which he was the instigator — his workmen presented him with a plaque for his fair treatment of his employees.[12]*

Koster was not an advocate of the total elimination of unions in San Francisco; rather, he felt that while unions might not be evil it was the radicals and the "outside agitators" who infiltrated the labor movement which turned unionism into a sour institution.[14] But he felt that shop conditions were better left to the benevolence of the employer than the capricious whim of the unions. Though he was not opposed to the basic principle of collective bargaining — after all *he* was using it — he remained against the activities of the unions. This might be likened to stating that one did not mind tortoises except for the shell. Koster, unfortunately, was unable to distinguish between local demands and nationwide objectives put forth by San Francisco unions and like so many of his contemporaries he also failed to make the critical distinctions among the various hues of radicalism and lumped Industrial Workers of the World, Socialists, Communists, Anarchists and labor organizers under the rubric "revolutionist."

*It is also interesting to note that the Argonaut, the vituperative, unofficial mouthpiece of the Law and Order Committee and the open shop campaign, was also a closed shop operation.[13]

To be successful in the drive for the open shop the Law and Order Committee needed two essential ingredients, financial independence and massive public support. The first was quickly attained. Within five minutes of the inception of the Committee it had been pledged $200,000 and by December of 1916 its treasury had more than a million dollars.[15]

Public support, however, was lukewarm. Though public sentiment might have favored the open shop the unions were still a potent economic force in San Francisco. Few businessmen were willing to generate a face-to-face confrontation with the unions unless they were absolutely sure of winning. The citizen of San Francisco who was neither a union member nor a businessman felt himself pinned. He could not help but be aware of the deteriorating industrial calm. The rising inflation affected him as much as any union member so he probably sympathized with the unions' position but he deplored the violence which was associated with the strikes. Any campaign by the Chamber of Commerce that might result in destruction of property or loss of human life was equally disagreeable. But the average citizen's greatest concern was that the open shop campaign would prolong the existing strikes and stir new ones into being. This was the person the Law and Order Committee had to sway.

The San Francisco and Bay Area newspapers were split over the open vs. closed shop controversy. Supporting the Committee were the conservative papers, William Randolph Hearst's San Francisco *Examiner* and the De Young *Argonaut*. The San Francisco *Call and Post* and the San Francisco *Chronicle* supported the Committee but with less regularity than the *Examiner* or *Argonaut*.

Of all the newspapers supporting the Committee, the *Argonaut*, which became its unofficial mouthpiece, was by far the most outspoken. In the early days of the open shop campaign when the businessmen were first beginning to push for action, the *Argonaut* pressed a reactionary position with gusto. In its July 15, 1916, issue it made the position of the Law and Order Committee clear: "Open Shop." Though many businessmen did not want to say those words publically, the *Argonaut* had no such compunction. Concerning the nobility of the open shop campaign the *Argonaut* stated:

> Let us hope that there will be no turning back on the part of the Chamber of Commerce and its supporters, no ebb in the enthusiasm with which this reform has begun.[16]

A month later the *Argonaut* again defended the campaign:

> Nothing not intrinsically right and just is demanded [in the fight for the open shop], nothing less will be accepted. War unremitting, consistent, legitimate, will be waged against conditions which have hampered and penalized business, destroyed confidence, driven forth industry, and shamed us in our hearts and before the world.[17]

The *Argonaut* made it clear that the fight for the open shop was a crusade and the issue was "not arbitratable."[18] Thus early in the campaign the demands for unconditional surrender were made. To say the least, this would hamper any attempts at arbitration.

Other journals, however, took a different stand on the open shop campaign. The *Coast Seaman's Journal*, the publication of the International Longshoremen's Association, mocked the open shop policy of the Chamber of Commerce as a "pitiful effort to defog the issue" of union unrest which was being carried on by a "plutocracy" whose "handmaid" was the *Argonaut*. There was no reason to fear however, *Journal* asserted; all the *Argonaut* and the Chamber of Commerce really do is prattle in "meaningless phraseology" anyway.[19]

There were also other journals critical of the Committee. Fremont Older, Progressive editor of the San Francisco *Bulletin*, felt that the Committee was nothing short of a "declaration of war" with labor and his paper collimated to that point of view.[20] The *Labor Clarion*, a Bay Area labor publication, opposed the Committee with religious consistency as did *The Blast*, an Anarchist publication edited by Alexander Berkman. While the *Labor Clarion* couched its assaults in literary style, *The Blast* was unrestrained. It clearly stated that a "slush fund" of one million dollars had been raised to "exterminate the unions."[21] The formation of the Law and Order Committee was nothing less than the employers' "throwing down the gauntlet to labor," an action that was "open war on organized labor."[22] But unlike other San Francisco newspapers *The Blast* welcomed the impending confrontation because there could never be "brotherhood between master and slave." Furthermore, that if the San Francisco unions wanted to be successful they must "*immediately declare a general strike.*"[24] Not only would this force the issue of the open vs. closed shop but it would awe the business community with the power of labor.

The *Labor Clarion*, whistling in the dark, printed a synopsis of the mass meeting with levity as though it were describing a gaggle of geese rather than businessmen:

> Some of the members of the Chamber of Commerce helped to keep the population of San Francisco and the bay districts highly amused during the past week by their ludicrous antics and loud boastings.
> Last Monday afternoon a mass meeting was held in the Merchants Exchange Building [the home of the Chamber of Commerce] at which the president of the Chamber of Commerce, Frederick J. Koster, announced that the meeting be a harmonious one, a program had been mapped out and only those known to be in sympathy with it would be allowed to speak.
> ....
> When the citizens of this city took up the morning papers at the breakfast table they were stirred to violent spasms of laughter by the announcement that this band of gold-loving, greed crazed braggers would put up $1,000,000 on the hazardous proposition of destroying organized labor in San Francisco. One old pioneer of the city who was familiar with the names and habits of the boasters was moved to such violent mirth that it became necessary to call in a physician to prevent a tragedy and restore him to normal. Truly, the labor haters added greatly to the gayety of the bay region.[25]

Private citizens also made their opposition to the Law and Order Committee known. Chester Rowell, editor of the San Francisco *Chronicle* and a personal friend of Koster, wrote Koster and warned him that the Committee was embarking on a "futile and dangerous policy."[26] Mayor James Rolph also viewed the formation of the Committee with displeasure. In a personal letter to Koster (see Appendix I), Rolph condemned the Committee as a horrible mistake on the part of the Chamber and contended that the mass meeting would only serve to entrench labor. Rolph stated:

> I cannot see wherein a meeting, ... can be of possible good; I do perceive wherein it may do much harm.... It is my profound conviction that the union of labor makes for the moral uplift of the country.... The system of collective bargaining is the essence of commercial progress.[27]

He closed the letter with a harsh insinuation: "As long as I am Mayor the Police Department will impartially enforce the Law."[28]

Despite the criticism, the Law and Order Committee began its campaign. The first order of business was to gain control of all drayage in the city. In the Waterfront strike of 1901 the control of the innercity transport companies had been vital to the success of the unions; in 1916 the Committee wanted to make it an arm of the Chamber of Commerce. On June 19 the Law and Order Committee circulated a document to the businesses of the city that, when signed, gave the Committee full power to make, break or extend contracts for the transportation of goods in San Francisco. This contract would be valid for three years. The Committee assured the businesses that its control of the drayage would not be used as a weapon unless it became "imperatively necessary to do so." However, "in case of necessity, ... the authority granted will be used."[29]

Within a few weeks the Committee had gained control of about 90 percent of all drayage in the city.[30] Although this power to stop the flow of goods to any particular business or area of the city was a potential economic bludgeon it was rarely used. More significantly it was used as a subtle threat to pressure recalcitrant business from siding with the unions. The most important fact, however, was that this power was denied the unions.

The Committee also used the courts. On July 13 for instance, it sought an injunction against the riggers and stevedores in an attempt to force them back to work. On July 17, before the case could be heard, the Riggers and Stevedores Local 38 voted to return to work, undoubtedly saving themselves from being ordered to do so by a judge.[31] Though the Committee claimed this as a victory, the true influence of the Committee in the courts had yet to be tested.

With the return of the riggers and stevedores to work, the Committee turned its attention to other matters. The ILA settlement affected only the longshoremen but still left the Bay and River Steamboat and Lumberyard strikes unresolved. The Bay and River Steamboat strike, though not specifically a San Francisco related problem, affected San Francisco commerce, giving the Committee a legitimate reason for entering negotiations. Through private meetings with the various steamboat owners an agreement was reached whereby the Riverboat Owners Association, represented by Captain A.E. Anderson, agreed to invest all powers of negotiation with the unions in the hands of the Law and Order Committee. As a result the Bay and River Steamboat Unions found themselves bargaining with the Committee, not their employers. This show of business solidarity was enough to break the strike and on July 19 the striking unions signed a settlement.[32] But the Riverboat Owners Association, like the Waterfront Employers Union before them, was now bound to follow where the Committee led.

Unlike the Waterfront strike and the Bay and River Steamboat strikes, the Lumberyard strike seemed to be holding. By late July a stalemate had been reached. Bowing to the pressure of the Committee, the Retail Lumber Dealers Association imposed a lockout of all union members and once again strikers and strikebreakers clashed along the San Francisco waterfront.

The Law and Order Committee also became involved in the Structural Steel strike — and later the Architectural Iron strike. On July 10 the structural steel industry in San Francisco had struck for an eight-hour day. More than fifty of the smaller structural steel firms in San Francisco had agreed to make the change from a nine-hour day but the ten largest refused to consider it.[33] With the backing of the Law and Order Committee and the San Francisco Building Trades Employers Association, on July 25 the firms delivered an ultimatum: if the unions did not return to work in three days an open shop would be instituted. It appeared that the ten firms were not looking for a settlement but for a pretext to force a lockout. When the unions refused to return a lockout was instituted.[34]

The collapsing of the Waterfront strike and the Bay and River Steamboat strike seemed to spell the end for the Committee. Though the Structural Steel and Lumberyard strikes were stalemated the Committee appeared to be a meteor disappearing over the horizon. The violence which had given it the legitimacy to begin its campaign had been resolved. Law and order had been maintained. The integrity of contracts had been upheld. The Committee's success was literally killing it. In paroxysms of joy the *Labor Clarion* noted:

> The million dollar bubble so noisily launched in the air about the bay by certain members of the San Francisco Chamber of Commerce has blown up and faded away just as those familiar with the tactics of the persons who started it on its journey predicted.[35]

But the Committee's base of support still remained. Although the general public had not warmed to the open shop campaign there was some sympathy for the passing of the organization. But the Committee was not dead yet and the *Labor Clarion's* prognosis was premature—24 hours premature.

The Radicals

One of the more annoying facts of life to the citizens of San Francisco in 1916 was the presence of radicals. The effect of these radicals on San Francisco was much the same of a half-dozen fleas on a dog. To the veterinarian the actual number of fleas is small; to the dog, he is infested.

Though many of the outspoken radicals were easily distinguishable, it was hard for many citizens to make a clear-cut distinction between a "radical" and a "labor organizer." Anarchists and Socialists, often associated with violence, sometimes joined with labor organizations for solidarity. Strikes were occasionally supported by Communists. Some unions, notably the Industrial Workers of World, were violent and assumed to be associated with Anarchists. To the business community in San Francisco it seemed as though the radicals had lined up with the unions against them.

Along with the open vs. closed shop violence which had plagued so many strikes in 1916, the businessmen were also forced to weather the harangue of the radical press. One of the most outspoken personalities within the radical community was Alexander Berkman, editor of the Anarchist publication *The Blast*. Since Berkman was the most visible personification of radicalism in San Francisco he took the brunt of the persecution for the group.

Berkman was the epitome of an Anarchist in both background and temperament. He was born in Vilna, Russia, in November of 1870, the son of a prosperous merchant. Later the Berkmans moved to St. Petersburg where young Alexander spent his formative years. His academic studies were marred by rebellion and culminated with his expulsion for an essay entitled "There is no God." Dissatisfied with life in Russia, Alexander left for the United States in 1886.[1]

Life in America did not live up to the young man's expectations. Rather than a haven for new ideas and philosophies, America, especially New York, seemed to Berkman to be just a newer sinkhole of the same myths he had left. Looking for a cause he fell under the spell of Johnathan Most, undoubtedly the most notorious Anarchist of that era. Through Most, Berkman met Emma Goldman, a woman whose name would be synonymous with Anarchism in the twentieth century.

In 1892 Berkman left his mark in American history. During the Homestead Steel Strike in Pittsburgh, Berkman saw in Henry Clay Frick the evil incarnate of all "employers." Under the naive assumption that the murder of Frick would spark a revolution, Berkman went to Pittsburgh to commit the first *attentat* — act of political terrorism — in American history. He also expected a martyrdom. Writing of Frick, Berkman speaks of both lives as if they were pawns in a chess game:

> Frick is the responsible factor in this crime [Homestead Strike]; he must be made to stand the consequences.... I will kill Frick, and of course I shall be condemned to death. I will die proudly in the assurance that I gave my life for the people. But I will die by my own hand.... Never will I permit our enemies to kill me.[2]

Berkman concluded that human life was "sacred and inviolate," but that Frick's death was "in no way to be considered as taking of life." Frick was "an enemy of the people" and his demise would be "splendid propaganda." This was the ultimate gambit.[3]

For several days Berkman shadowed Frick in Pittsburgh. Finally, on July 23, 1892, Berkman forced his way into Frick's office. When Berkman finally faced Frick:

> "Fr——," I began. The look of terror on his face strikes me speechless. It is the dread of the conscious presence of death. "He understands," it flashed through my mind. With a quick motion I draw the revolver. As I raise the weapon, I see Frick clutch with both hands the arms of the chair, and attempt to rise. I aim for his head. "Perhaps he wears armor," I reflect. With a look of horror he quickly averts his face, as I pull the trigger.[4]

He missed. Instantly the other man in the office tackled Berkman. On his way to jail a quick policeman pried Berkman's mouth open and removed an explosive capsule he had hidden in his mouth. Thus ended the *attentat*. The trial was quick and Berkman was sentenced to 22 years in prison.*

The most important lesson in the assassination attempt for

When Henry Clay Frick died he left a substantial sum of money to found the library at the University of Pittsburgh. Berkman died after a botched suicide attempt in Nice, France, left him suffering for hours.

Berkman was that he and Goldman had greatly misunderstood the attitude of the American workingman. He was stunned by the total disavowal of his act by American labor. Rather than a blow for labor, the *attentat* was viewed as yet another example of the violence attributable to the Anarchists. To the Homestead Strike it was like nailing the lid on the coffin.

When Berkman left prison in 1908 he was a changed man. Though his personal life was a shambles his zeal for the cause of Anarchism had not been diminished. He threw himself to work helping Goldman edit the publication *Mother Earth* in New York. By 1916 he had established himself in San Francisco and was publishing his own journal, *The Blast*.

The name of the periodical was unfortunate in that it left no doubt as to its purpose. To make the point crystal clear *The Blast* printed a poem by "Eric the Red" on the first page of the first edition, January 15, 1916, entitled "The Golden Rule":

> The Golden Rule has lived too long,
>   A myth from days of old,
> It tied the hands that, grim and strong,
>   Might stay the rule of Gold.
> Let now the shackles of the past
> Be shattered by a Blast.
>
> The rule of Gold — and Steel as well —
>   With aid of cant and creed
> Has made fair Earth a living Hell
>   Where only thieves succeed.
> The Golden Rule — Christ stands aghast —
> A leaf before the Blast.
>
> While Labor bleeds, hyenas laugh;
>   It thrills their putrid blood;
> They dance around their golden calf,
>   At peace with self and God.
> But he laughs best who laugheth last
> Beware the final Blast![5]

The Blast was more than just another radical publication. It was the focus for the radicals on the West Coast. Its format included arts and letters and was a potpourri of authors and subjects from abortion to Joe Hill; Tom Mooney to Tolstoi and Jack London to Eugene V. Debs. To the radicals *The Blast* was a forum, to the business community the message was clear:

> "The Blast does not stand for 'peace at any price.' It is in favor of war — war to the bitter end of the combined workers of the world against the despoilers."[6]
>
> *"Violence is a natural form of protest against injustice."*[7]
>
> "...our national honor is generally well hidden in our capitalist's pocket."[8]
>
> "Labor preparedness means to prepare the worker against their real and only enemy: the capitalist vampire that lives on their blood and marrow: to prepare to defend Labor against the constant growing rapacity and greed of the employer: to prepare to free Labor entirely from the bonds of wage slavery."[9]

Many San Franciscans were as upset with *The Blast*'s support of birth control as they were with its position on violence. In 1916, the tail end of the Victorian Age, talk of sex — let alone contraception — was tantamount to moral perversion. *The Blast* did not share this belief and freely published materials relating to birth control. Articles by Margaret Sanger, pioneer in the field of birth control advocacy, frequently appeared in *The Blast*. Pamphlets with such provocative titles as "What Every Girl Should Know," "Why the Poor Should Not Have Children," "Birth Control" and "The Right of the Child Not to Be Born" were advertised in *The Blast*.

The singular theme which consistently ran in *The Blast* was that organized labor was not "organized." Berkman summed up *The Blast*'s position in the March 1, 1916 edition:

> *The Blast* is a friend of labor, the friend of organized labor. But a satisfied silence is the bar to all progress, and *The Blast* intends, as a friend to labor, always to say exactly what it thinks, and it thinks there is not enough solidarity among labor.[10]

But Berkman was still misunderstanding American labor. The support of the Anarchists was more like cancer. Publicity in *The Blast* was bad publicity not matter what was said. To San Francisco labor Berkman was an embarrassment.

The other individual around whom the radical community rallied was William McDevitt. McDevitt, a Socialist, represented the more sedate revolutionaries. Unlike Berkman, McDevitt had received a college education. After receiving his L.L.D. from Georgetown University, McDevitt tried private practice but had become disillusioned. Gradually he had gravitated toward Socialism.

In 1905 McDevitt left the East Coast and moved to San Francisco. Within a short period of time he and other local radicals had organized a Socialist journal named *The Revolt*. Though the journal received a stirring sendoff from such notables as Jack London and Eugene V. Debs, it had a tenuous life. Enthusiasm could not cope with the financial burdens of publication and *The Revolt* folded in 1911. But it did survive long enough to allow excellent publicity for McDevitt's two ill-fated attempts to capture the mayorship of San Francisco in 1909 and 1911.[11]

Though he lost both times, the 1911 loss was significant. The Socialist Party polled a strong third that year and was granted a seat on the Board of Election Commissioners by the city charter.[12] McDevitt accepted the post, a move which understandably caused a great amount of bitterness among the various wings of the Socialist Party. While he was not busy with city affairs, McDevitt ran a small bookstore where he sold radical literature and sponsored a "People's Library."

McDevitt, to the radical and nonradical community, was a freak: a Socialist working within the framework that he despised. But McDevitt was aware that in the new era the bomb was *passé* and the ballot box was the ultimate weapon. It would take fifty years for the rest of America to learn the same lesson.

Public Backing
for the Committee

> *San Francisco is the most disgraced disrepicted city in all the world. It is the mecca of* Dynamiters, Thugs, Murders, Strikers, Anarchists, Emma Goldmans Ben Reihimans McNamaras *and all Else that is corrupt dangerous and wicked [*sic*].* — Dr. Paul Edwards to Mayor Rolph, July 25, 1916.[1]

The Law and Order Committee did not have long to wait for the backing of the public. On July 22, a Preparedness Day Parade had been scheduled. San Francisco, like many other American cities, held the parade as a symbol of its readiness for war. Although Woodrow Wilson's attitude toward joining the hostilities in Europe was lukewarm it was evident that this opinion would have to change. Across the nation the preparedness parades became the focus of the turbulent feelings of the communities in which they were staged. In San Francisco the parade was regarded as anti-German, antipacifist and anti-Wilson. (Wilson's neutrality irritated many San Franciscans. The most outrageous words were spoken on his stand on the sinking of cargo and passenger ships, an explosive issue in a maritime city such as San Francisco.) The parade also took on an anti-Spanish hue when a division of the march was given to some Spanish–American War veterans who announced that they intended to carry with them a "bullet-torn Flag" from their campaign.[2]

Whether by accident or design not a single division of the parade was given to labor. As an irritant to labor, the parade was led by Thornwell Mullally, a United Railroads director and an anathema to labor.[3] As the unions began to denounce the parade as a tool of management the parade began to take on an antiunion, pro-open shop tint. When the labor community finally condemned the parade it seemed to confirm the gnawing suspicion among businessmen that the unions were "anti-American" and associated with the radicals — at least ideologically. Thus the parade tended to widen the gap between business and labor and many feared that the celebration would be prelude to violence rather than unity.

Plans for the parade were given wide publicity. The festive mood of the parade, however, was broken by threats of violence. In the weeks preceding the march, and up to the moment that the Preparedness Day Parade actually began to move up Market Street, threats flooded the newspapers. Many were sent to prominent citizens who were responsible for the preparation of the parade. Over 200 threats, all lettered in the same hand, from the Employees Liberty League stated:

> Your extreme activity in promoting and glorifying militarism, marks you as the most vicious and dangerous "jingo" of all your brutal, greedy, thieving, and war-making class: and the immediate "extermination" of you and your evil class, is going to be the sole and "patriotic" duty of the EMPLOYEES LIBERTY LEAGUE.[4]

The Fresno *Morning Republican Daily* reported that some threats included a request to:

> Kindly ask the Chamber of Commerce to march in a solid body, *IF THEY WANT TO PROVE THEY ARE NO COWARDS.*[5]

Threats such as these tended to imply that the unions were contemplating violence. The police assured the public that they were investigating the threats but no progress was made in apprehending any culprits.

As early as July 8 an appeal had been made by labor leaders not to support the parade. In an appeal published in the San Francisco *Bulletin* workers were urged to boycott the parade:

> Workingmen, working women and working children.
> Organized labor through the Labor Council, the Building Trades Council, Waterfront Federation, as well as through action on the part of local unions have gone on record opposing the participation in the Preparedness Parade.
> Do not march.
> Do not let your employers coerce you into opposing the interests of the labor movement.
> Preparedness parades are engineered to boost the financial interest of the munitions trusts and allied industry.[6]

Among those who signed the appeal were such high ranking labor officials as Paul Scharrenberg, secretary of the State Federation of Labor and editor of the *Coast Seaman's Journal*, and O.A. Tveitmoe, secretary of the State Building Trades Council.[7]

Many labor leaders felt that the unions had no choice but to boycott the parade. Since the parade was led by Mullally, participation in the parade might tend some to believe that the unions were giving tacit consent to the open shop campaign. Secondly, if some unions marched and other unions did not it would appear that the labor front was not unified. Thirdly, any violence would carry the distinct odor of labor. The obvious course was not to march and labor chose to protest.

Representing the radical community, *The Blast* asserted that the Preparedness Day Parade was a sham. The true but unstated reasons for the parade were (1) to show the workers of San Francisco a united front against labor unrest and in favor of the open shop; (2) to show determination in the quest to attain American commercial dominance over South and Central America; (3) to show determination to conquer Mexico; (4) to protect Morgan interests around the world and (5) to aid in the exploitation of the world by a newly formed international trust [the United States of America?].[8] It would appear that *The Blast* considered Imperialism as the true impetus of the Preparedness Day Parade.

On July 21, the day before the Preparedness Parade, Fremont Older and members of the labor community — and members of the radical community — sponsored an Anti-Preparedness Day Rally. More than a protest, it was aimed at demonstrating to the business community that labor was united in their opposition to both the parade and the open shop. Among the speakers were Rudolph Spreckles, a San Francisco sugar manufacturer; Paul Scharrenberg, Fremont Older and William McDevitt. William A. Spooner, secretary of the Labor Council of Alameda, provided one of the livelier moments of the meeting when he announced that there were several detectives in the audience. An uproar followed and one of the detectives left.[9] Also among those in attendance was an official stenographer for the district attorney of San Francisco who recorded the speeches of Rudolph Spreckles and William McDevitt.[10] The overriding theme of the meeting was unity of labor; the main emphasis was that there should be no demonstrations of any kind against the parade. The unions were literally paranoid about a "possible frameup" for any acts of violence.[11]

Despite the threats and the Anti-Preparedness Day Rally, the parade was held. Extra policemen were stationed along the route as a crowd estimated at 50,000 San Franciscans and visitors gathered to watch the procession. The parade began at 1:30 where Market Streets meets the Embarcadero and moved slowly toward the financial district. Before it had progressed a mile, an abandoned suitcase at the corner of Market and Steuart streets* suddenly exploded, sending shrapnel into the crowd gathered on the sidewalk and divisions of the parade. When the smoke cleared, ten persons were dead and more than forty injured.

Horror was widespread. The next day the outrage of the public was reflected in the press. Throughout California and the rest of the United States the bombing made front page news for several days. In San Francisco the newspapers devoted huge sections to the bombing and listed in gruesome, intimate detail the carnage. Editorials on the bombing appeared on the editorial pages for weeks. William Randolph Hearst's San Francisco *Examiner* vituperatively pointed the editorial finger at the unions as the source of the outrage. The San Francisco *Call and Post* published a political cartoon entitled "Gloating" which pictured a three-headed serpent in a graveyard coiled around several headstones. One headstone read "killed by a bomb [illegible] PREPAREDNESS PARADE." The three heads were listed as "Fanatic," "Agitator" and "Agitator."[12] Though no one was specifically blaming the unions—yet—for the bombing, it was generally assumed that they were responsible.

The unions fought back weakly. With the exception of a literary assault by the *Coast Seaman's Journal* the union press was remarkably silent. The *Coast Seaman's Journal* labeled Hearst a "slanderous knave," "notorious profligate" and a "Malodorous politician and assassin of Character" who was not above using the outrage of the moment to proselytize:

> In true, matchless Hearstian style, cowardly and abhorrent murder on the streets of San Francisco is made the basis for a declaration that all those Americans who opposed militarism and war with Mexico are spreading "hate and disorder."[13]

The San Francisco radicals also felt the pressure created by the bombing. When Berkman heard of the carnage he said he hoped the public did not blame the Anarchists. When his secretary asked why

*This corner no longer exists.

the public should blame him he replied stoically "Because they always have."[14] This, however, did not keep him from printing that Hearst was guilty of "incitement to mob violence."[15] But the scoop was taken by the *International Socialist Review* which quoted a member of the Chamber of Commerce as stating "This is a fine chance for the open shop."[16] Whether this was propaganda or veracity the quote was uncomfortably close to reality.

In the wake of the bombing the Law and Order Committee suddenly became more aggressive. Much of this new vigor was a genuine outrage over the bombing. Many members, however, seemed to view the bombing of the parade as an extension of the violence on the docks. And many members undoubtedly felt that this would create a mandate for an end to the violence in San Francisco, giving the Committee the credit for being aware of the problem long before it erupted. The legitimacy of the Committee was now virtually guaranteed.

On July 26 the Law and Order Committee called a special mass meeting to protest the act of violence which had shaken the streets of San Francisco. The hysteria which had gripped the public was heightened even more when threats of violence against this mass meeting were publicized. These new threats, lettered in the same hand as those from the EMPLOYEES LIBERTY LEAGUE, contained threats against the July 26 meeting.[17]

In spite of the threats the meeting was packed. More than 6,000 San Franciscans, and so many policemen "that it seemed an armed camp," gathered to protest the bombing.[18] Koster spoke for the Law and Order Committee and announced that a $5,000 reward would be given for information leading to the conviction of those responsible for the explosion. Mayor Rolph also offered a reward and eloquently expressed his horror, and that of San Franciscans in general, over the bombing. Then the emphasis of the meeting began to take a subtle shift.

Koster stated that the bombing was an act of sabotage and declared that the fight against the person or persons responsible was not a partisan cause, but in "the common interest of every man in San Francisco."[19] To support the Law and Order Committee in restoring "law and order" Koster proposed the formation of a citizen's group to be called the Committee of One Hundred, a philosophical revival of the old vigilante committees of the previous century. The proposal was greeted with enthusiasm.

The next day the newspapers hailed the meeting as the rebirth of the Committees of Vigilance which had lain dormant for sixty years. The San Francisco *Call and Post* dubbed the Committee of One Hundred and the Law and Order Committee the "sons of the sires of 1856." Furthermore:

> The high resolve that consecrated their [Committees of Vigilance] work sixty years ago, recrudescent, spoke from the lips of the younger generation.... Times make the man. Leaders arise when the occasion is large. There was a Coleman in 1856; there is a Koster today.[20]

The Committee of One Hundred was a magnificent move. In one stroke Koster had harnessed the mandate, expanded his visible public support, put the police and the city administration on the defensive and garnered the glories for the Committee's apparent foresightedness. When the Committee of One Hundred was chosen (see Appendix II), it included a substantial chunk of the most powerful men in San Francisco.[21] In terms of power, wealth and prestige such a collection of men could never exist again in any city in the United States. These men *were* the city of San Francisco. They controlled the business of the city. They dominated the social register. They represented San Francisco by their mere presence anywhere in the world. The list included such notable families as Ghirardelli, Buckbee, Crocker, Fleishhacker, Giannini, Lilienthal, Sproule, Sutro, Matson, Dollar and Spreckles. The only notable absences were Mayor Rolph, Fremont Older and any representatives of the labor community.

The Committee of One Hundred, which never had a hundred members, was the best front the Law and Order Committee could devise. The Committee of One Hundred was a figurehead organization with no power to express a point of view. Some of the members did not even know they had been nominated and many others were already members of the Chamber of Commerce and supporters of the Law and Order campaign. The Committee of One Hundred displayed its impotence at its first and only meeting when it went on record supporting the Law and Order Committee for a period of two years and then ceased to exist.[22]

The Committee of One Hundred was also meant to awe not only the unions but the city administration and the police. The unions were convinced that they had been fighting these men for years and were thus unconcerned with the membership of the

Committee of One Hundred. City officials might be tempted to think otherwise. With such a collection of power and prestige consolidated on the side of the Law and Order Committee civil servants might be expected to restrain their efforts where the unions were involved. Especially vulnerable was Mayor Rolph since he was an elected official. The police, already on the defensive since they had not prevented the Preparedness Day bombing, also might feel pressure with such an illustrious company watching their every move.

But the ironic twist of fate was that the Committee of One Hundred could not express its view opposing the Law and Order Committee. Thus it was inextricably tied to the Law and Order Committee and bound to follow where it led. Just as credit for the excellence of the Law and Order Committee shone on the Committee of One Hundred, so must the guilt of one besmirch the other.

In the aftermath of the bombing the unions maintained a low profile. With the Law and Order Committee pressing aggressively for the open shop the unions felt constricted. A strike laced with any violence would immediately focus the outrage of the public directly on the unions. Quite abruptly the antiunion sentiment which had been more of a floating suspicion than a directed accusation exploded into a public wrath when two labor organizers, Thomas J. Mooney and Warren K. Billings, were arrested for the bombing. The fact that the first was a Socialist and the second had been previously jailed on a suspected dynamiting charge did little to quell the public furor. In the interest of self preservation the unions were careful to disavow any affiliation with Mooney or Billings. The *Labor Clarion* stated:

> these persons [insinuating Mooney and Billings] with IWW proclivities never produce anything but trouble and bring on disaster whenever they appear, whether in union circles or elsewhere.[23]

Fremont Older, who usually associated himself with the underdogs, quite succinctly repudiated Mooney: "Let the son-of-a-bitch hang!"[24] Though the Law and Order Committee was not as vocal as the unions in this matter, it did admit that Mooney and Billings were "not and have never been union labor men."[25] This, however, did not stop the Committee from exploiting the Mooney–Billings affair for three years.

For the next three years the Mooney–Billings trials would occupy much of the Committee's time. Closely associating itself with the prosecution of the two, the Committee was unfortunately party to many legal shenanigans and extralegal tactics which marred the prosecution and turned the entire case into a carnival. To this day the Mooney–Billings case is a *cause célèbre* for American labor.*

The Law and Order Committee realized that the moment to press for the open shop had arrived. With the deliberation of a chess master sensing a critical breach in the opponent's defense, the Committee aggressively pressed its advantage. Though neither Mooney nor Billings was associated with any of the strikes the Committee had entered, the bombing was an excellent stalking horse. San Franciscans were demanding retribution for the outrage. With a finesse born of expedience the Committee bound the violence along the waterfront to the Preparedness Day bombing. Mooney and Billings were the critical bridge between these marginally related episodes.

The Committee entered the Structural Steel and Culinary strikes with vigor. For the struck steel firms, the Committee provided strikebreakers and armed guards. It was also liberal in supplying financial support to help the employers recoup. Publicly the Committee claimed that it was only aiding the employers in the "maintenance of law and order."[26]

The Committee was also aggressive in dealing with striking culinary workers. Originally the strike had been called on July 15 to back the Culinary Union's demand for an eight-hour day. The San Francisco Restaurant Employer's Association (SFREA) had refused and, with the consent of the Committee, instituted an industry-wide lockout.[27] Violence, including the throwing of food and stinkbombs, erupted as several thousand culinary workers were thrown into the streets. The Committee capitalized on the violence and entered the strike publicly. In a statement released by Koster the Committee made its position clear:

> The strike of the cooks, cooks' helpers and waiters ... affords a splendid example of just the conditions in San Francisco that the law and order committee of the Chamber of Commerce and the Chamber of Commerce itself is striving to remedy.
>
> The law and order committee stands back of the San Francisco Restaurant Employer's Association in this situation. The Committee has at all times been in close touch with the progress of negotiations between the culinary workers and the employers.[28]

**See Frost's* The Mooney Case *and Gentry's* Frame-Up *in the Bibliography.*

(Note that the statement includes the Chamber of Commerce in the first paragraph but places all of the emphasis on the Law and Order Committee in the second paragraph.) Help for the SFREA included the hiring of detectives and guards to protect the restaurants which had opened on an open shop basis.[29]

The SFREA received more help than it needed. In accordance with the agreement with the Committee, the SFREA proceeded to channel all protest and court actions through the Committee. The Committee aided by distributing "open shop coupons" which were only good in open shop restaurants.[30] The receipts from the sales of these coupons was turned over to the SFREA. To help the citizens of San Francisco distinguish between the open shop and closed shop establishments the SFREA placed special open shop plaques in the windows of the struck businesses. These plaques read "This house is conducted as an open shop. We do not discriminate against union or nonunion men."[31] Prominently displayed in the windows of the open shop restaurants, they left no doubt in the public's mind which shops were union and which were open shop.

At first the culinary workers seemed to be doing well. Though the open shop coupons had been widely distributed most were not used. The closed shop establishments, on the other hand, nearly doubled their business in the early days of the strike. But behind the scenes the pressure began to mount. The Committee, not content to be just a back-up organization, began to circulate a petition that would make picketing within the city limits illegal.[32] Considering the violence which had plagued the strikes since June 1, the Committee expected this to pass easily. Then, if the culinary strike could not be won with detectives, strikebreakers and guards, the Committee would use the ballot box and the courts.

In the face of this new threat the unions were somewhat impotent. As Berkman had so aptly noted in *The Blast*, the Committee would not be defeated on a dollar for dollar basis.[33] If the Culinary strike was to be won at all it would have to be won quickly. In a mass labor meeting on August 17, 1916, John A. O'Connell, secretary of the San Francisco Labor Council, reiterated this point and urged the workers to put "pep and ginger" into the strike.[34] Time was critical.

But the unions were no match for the Law and Order Committee. Gradually the economic pressure exerted by the Committee began to be felt in the strike. Those to feel the pressure first were the closed shop restaurants. A typical incident was reported in both the

Coast Seaman's Journal and the *Labor Clarion*. Both papers described the experience of the California Cafeteria which had broken away from the SFREA and repudiated the open shop. Within three days of its defection the California Cafeteria found it impossible to buy food:

> On the third day after I had reopened my place of business as a union house [closed shop] the driver for G.H. Roberts, a dealer in corned beef, informed me that one cafeteria owner had returned his order of corned beef because he had sold me [California Cafeteria] meat, and that if he continued to furnish me with corned beef he would find that all open shop restaurant owners would refuse to patronize him.[35]

The Committee also used the courts. Through its legal counsel of Metson, Drew and McKenzie the Committee pressed for restraining orders against the striking unions. By the end of the strike more than 200 orders had been given. The issuing of these orders particularly irritated the unions since it was in violation of a tacit precedent set into motion several years previously. At that time it had been arranged with several Superior Court judges that no restraining orders would be issued before a special hearing had been called. Judge Hunt, the Superior Court Judge in 1916, did not feel bound by this precedent and issued restraining orders as they were requested.[36]

The success of the Committee in the Superior Court, however, was not repeated elsewhere. In the police courts the Committee created more problems than it solved. With an eye to putting pressure on police court judges, the Committee had installed a special prosecutor to aid in the prosecution of labor cases. This special prosecutor, Porter Ashe — and his compeer from the SFREA, Arthur Joel — created so much controversy that they were expelled from the court room.[37] Subsequent investigations into their activities revealed that they had undoubtedly framed at least one defendent and then tried to cover up the case.[38] Incidents such as this did little to enhance the image of the Law and Order Committee in the eyes of the public.

As the Culinary Strike dragged on it became clear that the only way the Committee and the SFREA could weather the strike was to have enough money and manpower to outlast the unions. Money was not a problem; manpower was. Since there was not an adequate supply of scab labor in San Francisco, the Committee began recruiting strikebreakers from other cities. Often this labor came from as far away as Chicago, St. Louis or New Orleans.[39] As the scabs arrived, San Franciscans braced for the impending labor disputes which traditionally led to violence.

In an attempt to forestall any violence, Mayor Rolph entered the rapidly deteriorating stalemate and took an active part in the disputes. Hopeful that the primary problem in San Francisco was one of communication, Rolph began to apply his prestige as a catalyst toward a settlement. On August 1 Rolph sent a letter to the San Francisco Chamber of Commerce, San Francisco Labor Council, San Francisco Building Trades Council and the Waterfront Worker's Federation suggesting that an arbitration committee be convened to help settle, among other strikes, the Structural Steel and Culinary Strikes. Rolph's proposal was for an arbitration board composed of 15 members; five from the Chamber of Commerce and the business community, five from the labor community and five from the clergy of San Francisco. The members of the clergy would be chosen by the Most Reverend Archbishop Edward J. Hanna because, in Rolph's opinion, there was "no other member of the community who possesses, in such a unique degree, the confidence of all classes."[40] It was Rolph's opinion that the arbitration committee was critical because San Francisco:

> would take only a little more strain to precipitate one of those wasteful and distressful struggles between Labor and Capital which settles nothing, brings no good to anyone and divides a community for years.[41]

By August 14 the San Francisco Labor Council, San Francisco Building Trades Council and the Waterfront Worker's Federation had answered in the affirmative.[42] On August 16 the Law and Order Committee gave its answer. The reply, released by Koster to the press, was a blistering attack on the labor unions. He asserted that the position of the Law and Order Committee and the Chamber of Commerce was in opposition to any arbitration committee. The Chamber and the Committee refused to be a "party to any arbitration which would have the authority to compromise."[43] Furthermore, the Committee refused to "consent to cloud the plain issue which this community [was] eager to face."[44]

Support for the Committee's position was not long in coming.

The *Argonaut* backed the Committee's position and stated that any arbitration committee would be a sham unless the forces of "nonunion labor" were represented; the open shop was either right or wrong and the community should decide the merits of the struggle. Thus any compromise would merely be postponing the inevitable confrontation.[45]

William Sproule, president of the Southern Pacific Railroad, also expressed himself on the issue of arbitration. In a personal letter to Mayor Rolph (addressed on company stationery with an inside address and a notation that it had been dictated), Sproule made it clear that the business community represented the "backbone and sinew of the city." The bulk of the letter was innocuous but one of the last paragraphs was leading:

> My interest in addressing you is not personal to me or in direct relation to anything I represent. It is the word of one citizen to another. A helping hand from each of us will be helpful to all, to our interest in common, and to your interest.[46]

Rolph was not pleased with the rejection of his arbitration scheme. He had placed his reputation and influence on the line and the Chamber of Commerce and the Law and Order Committee had publicly, and unconditionally, snubbed him. In essence the Committee had told him to stay out of San Francisco labor disputes. In a letter to the city newspapers Rolph announced the abandonment of his arbitration scheme because the Committee was "so obviously right that the issues are not disputable."[47]

But in spite of Koster's alleged opposition to the arbitration committee, the Law and Order Committee made a magnificent counterplay. It arranged for its own arbitration committee with the unions! If the Committee had refused to arbitrate under any conditions it would have appeared as if they did not care for a settlement. Rolph's arbitration committee was unacceptable because it might compromise the open shop campaign. Thus, on August 17, despite previous public statements to the contrary, the Law and Order Committee sponsored a meeting between labor and management.[48]

But there were several important differences between the meeting actually held and that proposed by the mayor. Rolph, who would have played a key role in his arbitration scheme, was absent from the Committee's meeting. Secondly, Hanna played only a minor role in the Committee's arbitration scheme whereas with the Mayor's plan he would have been a major participant. This was a premeditated, direct slice at Hanna's credibility. Finally, rather than meeting in a neutral location—originally the mayor's chambers—the meeting was actually held in the law offices of Metson, Drew and McKenzie.[49]

As could be expected the meeting accomplished nothing. But, from the Committee's point of view, two important aspects of the meeting were successful. Firstly, an arbitration meeting had been held and to the public it appeared that the Committee was indeed trying to reach some agreement with the unions. Secondly, it was an important lulling influence on the unions for the preceding week when Charles Evans Hughes, candidate for the presidency of the United States, planned to be campaigning in San Francisco.

Charles Evans Hughes in San Francisco

With the exception of the single day Charles Evans Hughes campaigned in San Francisco, the Law and Order Committee had little lasting effect on San Francisco or California politics. The open shop theory was the prime justification for its existence and the heyday of the Robber Barons was at an end. Unionization was about to come of age. In two decades the Mooney–Billings affair would be a footnote in a book of California history or a short aside in an upper division class in Western history. But the Committee overestimated its importance in San Francisco and at a critical moment made a decision which was to have international ramifications.

The roots of Charles Evans Hughes' defeat sank deep in the soil of American politics. Since the turn of the century the left wing of the Republican Party had felt that it was being consistently disenfranchised by its more conservative colleagues. Ample proof of the wave of reformism in America seemed to be evident in the growing popularity of Eugene V. Debs. Though Debs stood on the far left fringe of the American political spectrum, his ballet box popularity had risen more than ninefold from 1900 to 1912 and many reformers looked at Debs as the harbinger of a new American enlightenment.[1]

In 1912 came a catalyst. Dissatisfied with the policies of his political protégé, Theodore Roosevelt led a coterie of left wing Republicans out of the party to form the Bull Moose Party—more commonly known as the Progressive Party. But the Progressive experiment was a badly timed fling at splinter politics. Fueled more by crusading fervor than electorate support the Progressive Party did little but insure the success of the Democrats.

The ensuing lopsided electoral victory of the Democrats seemed to indicate that the Republican Party was moribund. Though Woodrow Wilson took only 41.9 percent of the popular vote, he captured a whopping 81.9 percent of the electoral vote. This was the greatest electoral victory since Lincoln trounced General McClellan in 1864. The Progressives, running Roosevelt as their candidate, took 27.4 percent of the popular vote and 16.6 percent of the electoral vote while their erstwhile party took only 23.2 percent of the popular vote and a mere 1.5 percent of the electoral vote.[2] Thus ended 16 years of Republican domination of the White House.

But the Republican's case was not terminal. Roosevelt, head of the hydra-like Progressives, gradually realized the defectors were reformers, not political men. Rather than forming the nucleus of a new political persuasion, the bolters had proven to be headstrong and dedicated to "well-meant extravagances" rather than party organization.[3] Gradually, as the nation's attention shifted from domestic infighting to international alliances, Roosevelt's allegiance aligned with Republican interests. Roosevelt's return to the Party marked the resurrection of the Republican Party and the erosion of Progressive influence. But the wounds of 1912 had only begun to heal by 1916.

In the months preceding the Republican National Convention a great concern was voiced within the party for a candidate who could represent both moieties yet was unscathed by the fiasco of 1912. Charles Evans Hughes met the requirements. As the former reforming governor of New York, Hughes would be acceptable to the returning Progressives. His support by the conservatives seemed assured by his status as a member of the United States Supreme Court. Of greatest importance, however, was Hughes' political aloofness since his appointment to the Supreme Court bench in 1910 thus relieving him of any culpability for the 1912 Republican debacle.

Soon after his nomination Hughes moved quickly to consolidate his support with both wings of the Party. Meeting with Roosevelt and William Howard Taft — on separate occasions — he enlisted their support for the building Republican victory. With the naïveté reminiscent of a myopic scholar, Hughes felt that the Progressive Party could be wooed back to Republican ranks simply by dining with Roosevelt. What he failed to realize was that Progressivism was a grassroots movement which had precipitated national repercussions, not vice versa. It would be on the local level, not the national level, where the wooing would be necessary. Hughes' education was to be expensive.

The Democrats were also having difficulties. Domestic concerns which had dominated the Wilson years were rapidly being dwarfed as the international storm clouds gathered. As the war in Europe changed from the initial burst of patriotic fervor to the protracted attrition of tench warfare, American found itself being inexorably drawn toward the vortex. Though many Americans felt that American soldiers would eventually have to fight in Europe,

President Wilson appeared reluctant to take a stand. His campaign slogan, "He kept us out of war," satisfied few Americans as prowar sentiment began to bud across the United States.

As Hughes approached California on the western swing of his campaign tour, the political storm clouds darkened. Though the demise of the Progressive Party on the national level was apparent, in California the Progressives were a rational force if lacking a guiding authority. Both major parties recognized that California would be a key state in the election; thus successful wooing of the Progressive sentiment was imperative.[4] In California the Progressive sentiment was embodied in the governor, Hiram Johnson, who had become titular head of the Progressives with the return of Roosevelt to the Republican fold. Under the impression that support by Johnson could be equated as support by the Progressives, Hughes made a special effort to gain the support of the Governor.

Johnson and Hughes had conferred briefly after Hughes' nomination at which time Johnson had assured Hughes of his support. On July 8, 1916, Hughes attempted to solidify his support with the Progressives. When Johnson officially opened his campaign for senator on the Progressive ticket—running against a Republican, Willis Booth—Hughes wired Johnson at the California Progressive Conference:

> The national aims to which we are devoted are so vitally important that I earnestly hope there may be that strong and effective cooperation which will assure their achievement. I desire a reunited Party as the essential agency of national progress, a Party drawing to itself the liberal sentiment of a quickened nation.... We are not divided in our ideals, let us work together to attain them.[5]

But the Republican–Progressive coalition in California was more of a union of two contestants involved in a tug-of-war with a chasm between them. The old guard Republicans viewed the Progressives as upstarts who had shattered the party for a useless exercise in political science which appeared more as a sophisticated tantrum than a long shot with a dark horse. The Progressives, on the other hand, looked upon the old guard Republicans as the last gathering of the dinosaurs at the La Brea tarpit. For the Progressives the new religion was reform and it was being undermined in California by the "Big Business" interests; in California, specifically, the Southern Pacific Company. Evil incarnate to the Progressives was William H. Crocker with his odious connection to the Southern Pacific machine. Crocker was the Republican National Committeeman and one of the two men representing the Republican Party who were to meet with the Progressives to iron out details of Hughes' visit.

In the ensuing effort to create an amiable tour for Hughes, the Progressives were represented by Chester H. Rowell, editor of the San Francisco *Chronicle* and Progressive National Committeeman. In addition to Crocker the Republicans were represented by State Central Committee Chairman Francis B. Keesling. Both sides were equal in their desire to see that the other side did not receive any political advantage from the Hughes visit. Rowell proposed that Johnson introduce Hughes in San Francisco inasmuch as the Republican steering committee had made a promise to support the Governor in his bid for senator. Crocker said that he had heard of no such promise and flatly stated he had one overriding concern: to defeat Johnson in favor of Booth. When Rowell wired William R. Willcox, Hughes' campaign manager, for confirmation of the promise given by the Republican steering committee, Willcox chose to ignore the fact that any consideration had been given Johnson. Willcox effectively destroyed Rowell's credibility in the eyes of Crocker and Keesling and confirmed Rowell's suspicion that the old guard had no intention of dealing honorably with the Progressives.[6]

When it became painfully evident that no agreement could be reached, it was suggested to Hughes by Crocker that the California swing be canceled—at least until after the primaries. But Hughes, adamant in his determination to tour California, felt that it was essential to a Republican victory for him to tour the state and make amends with Johnson. Furthermore, his campaign schedule placed him in the Far West only once as he intended to spend the closing weeks of the campaign in the East. To slight California would have been politically unwise.[7]

By the end of July it appeared as if the old guard Republicans were in complete charge of the Hughes visit and were preparing to make the most of his political patronage. Since the confrontation with Rowell, Willcox sent a wire stating that "he thought it proper" for Johnson to preside at either the rally in San Francisco or the rally in Los Angeles. Crocker and Keesling naturally opposed this idea in toto. In the eleventh hour an attempt to salvage the rapidly deteriorating California visit, Willcox wired Crocker and Rowell to meet with the candidate in Portland on August 16:

> Have telegram from Manager of Hughes' train which suggests you [Crocker] and Rowell meet train in Portland on Wednesday, August sixteenth, and travel with Governor Hughes to San Francisco and to withhold final arrangements about Chairman until then, unless you have come to an agreement.[8]

Rowell agreed to meet with Hughes. Crocker, however, either assuming that the Republicans were in charge or jumping the gun on the arrangements wired:

> Replying to your telegram today, all arrangements for California have been completed.[9]

Thus the chasm between the two organizations widened further.

To try to break the stalemate, both parties were instructed to meet with the candidate. Rowell joined the campaign train first and urged Hughes to give Johnson recognition in California. But Hughes, still trying to stay out of local politics, declared that he intended to remain aloof from the Republican-Progressive split in California. Rowell was appalled at Hughes' naïveté. Later, in a letter to Roosevelt, Rowell commented that if Hughes was actually unaware of the situation in California then "he was the only person on the train" who did not understand the explosive possibilities of the schism.[10]

Crocker and Keesling, despite Crocker's statement that he had no need of meeting with Hughes, boarded the campaign train in Gerber, Oregon. In private talks with Frederick M. Davenport, a close friend of Hughes, Crocker insisted that Hughes be kept away from Johnson at all costs. It was Crocker's personal contention that Johnson did not have much of a chance against the reunited party and any connection between Johnson and Hughes would bode ill for Republican chances—Hughes or Booth. The upshot of the meeting was the granting of the Hughes tour to the hands of the old guard Republicans. The Progressives, it would seem, were out in the cold.[11]

This was another in a series of tragic blunders which haunted Hughes throughout his California visit. By acquiescing to the demands of Crocker and Keesling, Hughes was literally asking the Progressives to nail the lid on his political coffin. Hughes had absolutely no conception of the depths of the hatred between the Progressives and the old guard Republicans in California. The juggernaut to disaster had begun.

The San Francisco rally was a Progressive disaster. Keesling introduced Crocker and Crocker introduced Hughes. Rowell sat on the stage silent and impotent. Hughes, "still hoping that he could ride through California with one foot on the back of the Elephant and the other on the back of the Bull Moose," attempted to make his position crystal clear:[12]

> I come as the spokesman of a reunited Republican Party to talk to you of national issues—with local differences I have no concern.[13]

To the Progressives this statement was the kiss of death. In essence Hughes was totally discounting the California Progressives as a viable political party. Moreover, Hughes appeared to be disenfranchising Johnson in favor of his Republican opponent. The Progressives, many of whom were in favor of a Hughes administration in the White House, were appalled.

The next day, August 19, Rowell was quoted as saying that the rally had been a "frost." Hughes, Rowell contended, was "abandoning the Progressives to the wolves" in favor of his own election. Then, stating that his wife was about to undergo surgery, Rowell resigned from the Hughes entourage. His vacancy was not filled.[14]

August of 1916 was not a good month for politicians. With less than three months to go before the people of the United States cast their ballots, both candidates suddenly found themselves involved in more controversy. In Washington, D.C., Woodrow Wilson was desperately trying to stave off a nationwide railroad strike. After a series of communications with both parties, Wilson met with 31 railroad presidents on August 18, the day Charles Evans Hughes was in San Francisco, in hopes that some settlement could be reached. The presidents were unmoved as were their compeers who met with the President 72 hours later. After six more days of fruitless negotiations, Wilson decided to try to press a settlement through Congress. After a rancorous fight in the House and Senate a bill passed granting the eight-hour day. The new law was named the Adamson Act after the man who had pressed it through the House, Chairman William C. Adamson. But the passage of the bill had been close; so close in fact that Wilson, anticipating failure, had recalled 15,000 troops from the Mexican border to be on hand if they were needed to maintain law and order should the strike occur.

Hughes, among many others, denounced the signing of the

Adamson Act as a campaign gift to the unions. Others conceded that the eight-hour day was a long overdue reform. But in San Francisco, the bill was greeted with cheering—loudest it would seem from the striking structural steel and culinary workers.

Hughes was also having problems. In August of 1916, San Francisco was undoubtedly the most dangerous city in the United States for a presidential candidate. A nationwide railroad strike was in the making, San Francisco was in the midst of a labor-management war, the Mooney-Billings trials were in full swing, the trial of William McDevitt was being held, the open shop campaign was still gathering strength—and enemies—and the Progressives were still not sympathetic to the idea of a "reunited" Republican Party. And, of all the cities in the United States, San Francisco—a city dominated by labor since the turn of the century—was *not* the place to make a *faux pas* with labor.

But, being a guest of the California Republican State Central Committee, represented by Keesling and Crocker, Hughes was bound to abide by their itinerary. This was the fatal factor. Though Keesling knew that San Francisco was in the midst of a culinary strike, among others, he made no attempt to shield Hughes from adverse publicity. On the contrary, it appears that he forced Hughes to attend a luncheon at a struck restaurant.[15]

Hughes had been agonizing over this situation for more than a week. In Portland he had been advised to cancel the banquet rather than run the risk of offending the San Francisco labor unions. Hughes had rejected this option and stated that he would attend the luncheon—otherwise it could be insinuated that the candidate "lacked courage."[16]

This, however, was a dangerous move. Discretion being the better part of valor, it would have been a safe move for Hughes to become conveniently ill. Often a diplomatic illness is strategically more decisive than a good offense. Furthermore, it was political suicide for Hughes to even *appear* to be sympathetic to the open shop campaign, let alone be known as a sympathizer of the Law and Order Committee. With the benefit of hindsight it would appear that only sheer madness could explain Hughes' failure to bow out of the engagement.

When Hughes arrived in San Francisco he sent his personal manager, Charles Farnham, to talk to Hugo Ernst, president of the striking Cooks and Waiters Union.[17] The delicacy of the situation did not impress Ernst, who responded that the Commercial Club had "insulted organized labor" in San Francisco by forcing the issue of the open shop. (Ernst had also engendered the face-off between labor and management during the Hughes visit by issuing a public letter in the San Francisco *Bulletin* which, in an attempt by the unions to gain patronage from the Hughes tour, insisted that Hughes publicly repudiate the open shop campaign.) Ernst, however, was willing to make a deal. He would delay the strike but the open shop plaque in the window of the Commercial Club would have to be removed "while our men are serving the luncheon."[18] This conveniently left the next move to the San Francisco Commercial Club.

Why the plaque was not removed has not been recorded. It can be safely assumed that the Commercial Club conferred with the Law and Order Committee. The Committee undoubtedly realized that with Hughes in San Francisco there would be nationwide publicity for the open shop campaign which in turn could turn the open shop into a nationwide campaign. Not only would the publicity insure support in San Francisco but it would make the Committee a celebrity with other management groups throughout the United States.

Furthermore, since the Law and Order Committee was considering sending representatives to Sacramento to carry the campaign onto the state level, this publicity would be an excellent springboard to launch the new, statewide campaign. And, moreover, quite confident that Hughes would win the election without San Francisco, it was probably decided that the plaque should stay. The Commercial Club concurred and the plaque remained in the front window.

At this point Farnham was desperate. When he asked Keesling to move the banquet to another location, Keesling replied that it was too late since all of the arrangements had been made. When Farnham asked Crocker, a member of the club, to persuade the Commercial Club to remove the plaque, Crocker "shrugged his shoulders and said he could do nothing."[19] It appeared that the local labor Republicans were more concerned with winning a minor skirmish with local labor unions than they were with winning the presidency of the United States.

Despite the efforts of Hughes to play down the significance of his meal at the Commercial Club there was an inflamed protest by the labor community. When the plaque was not removed from the window of the club, Ernst refused to allow the cooks and waiters to serve the luncheon. In a letter to the Commercial Club Ernst wrote:

> The Waiter's Union has received an order for sixty-five union men to serve the luncheon this afternoon.
>
> We thank you very much for your consideration in allowing our membership a chance to earn a few dollars; but inasmuch as you have organized your place with an open shop card at the request of the Restaurant Men's Association, with whom you have no logical affiliation,* we are forced to prohibit our members from serving at said Hughes luncheon.
>
> Had Mr. Hughes taken advantage of the opportunity afforded him to make a statement on his attitude on the open shop question which is agitating organized labor at this time and had he declared himself for the closed shop, we would not be forced to take this drastic action.
>
> We are sorry that this concerns one of the best known Americans. We are sorry to be forced to do this thing but the Commercial Club, its officers and members must suffer the responsibility for their unrighteous war upon the workers connected with our industry.[20]

The next day the labor press scorched Hughes as an enemy of labor and a cohort of the Law and Order Committee. The coverage made a mockery of the words Hughes had spoken less than 24 hours previously. In a single meal Hughes had labeled himself as a supporter of the open shop campaign not only in San Francisco but across the nation.

But the bad press did not seem to concern either the local business community or national Republican leaders. Unfortunate the incident may have been; fatal it was not. Wall Street was still betting on Charles Evans Hughes as the next president of the United States. The sentiment of the San Francisco business community can best be summed up by quoting from a letter by Rudolph Spreckles of Spreckles Sugar to James D. Phelan, Democratic senator from California and a personal friend of Spreckles. Spreckles asked Phelan to "telegraph me if you [want?] to bet a $2500 against $4000 on Hughes [sic]."[21] Even the San Francisco *Chronicle* seemed to concede that Hughes had the election in the bag. On August 20, the day after

---

*The Commercial Club was not strictly a restaurant. When it served a luncheon, it had to send out for cooks, waiters and food. It would appear that the Commercial Club was asking for some sort of reaction from the unions.

the fiasco at the Commercial Club, the *Chronicle* printed a story entitled "Hughes Leaves San Francisco with Fall Ballot Won."[22]

The *Argonaut* felt that the situation was secure enough to lambaste the unions for their walkout at the banquet. In the August 26 issue—the first edition of the weekly to appear after the Hughes luncheon—the *Argonaut* printed a stinging tirade of the unions. The *Argonaut* insisted that the walkout of the culinary workers was characteristic of the

> shamelessness of that species of unionism under which San Francisco had long suffered, and which had been a blight, not less upon our [San Franciscans'] dignity than upon our prosperity.[23]

Though the San Francisco visit may have been the fatal episode in the Hughes campaign, it must be remembered that the San Francisco fiasco was an alienation of union sentiment and not necessarily Progressive sentiment. It almost seemed as if Hughes had been destined to alienate the labor community. His disastrous meal was just the beginning. Hughes continued to stir resentment when he attacked the Adamson Act as a "shocking abandonment of principle" and continued to harass the eight-hour day throughout the rest of his campaign.* With several of the San Francisco strikes directly related to the eight-hour day, this stand was not likely to endear Hughes any further with the labor community.

As if the California visit had not been bad enough, Hughes managed to make one more major gaffe, this time in Long Beach. By coincidence both Hughes and Governor Johnson were in the same hotel at the same time but Hughes claimed he was not advised of this fact. As Johnson had not been invited to any Republican gathering with Hughes this would have been an opportune moment for the two men to hold an impromptu news conference. Such a meeting might have soothed over the tensions of the San Francisco fiasco.

Johnson claimed that the hotel manager knew the two men were in the hotel but did nothing to tell Hughes. Keesling claimed he did not know of the coincidence. Johnson, not wishing to appear as a publicity hog, merely sat in his hotel and allowed the candidate to leave.

*President Woodrow Wilson signed the Adamson Act into law on September 2, 1916, thus stopping a nationwide railroad strike. Many felt that this was a campaign gift to the unions.[24]

When Hughes discovered his error he was horrified. Immediately after he had received word of his slight he sent Farnham and Keesling—an odd choice—back to Long Beach to apologize to Johnson. Why he did not use the telephone for a more personal apology is not known. Late that night as Hughes was boarding the train for San Diego he told Davenport, "If I had known Johnson was in that hotel, I would have seen him if I had to kick the door down."[25]

If the California tour had not been bad enough already, Keesling aggravated Johnson by suggesting that the Governor accompany Hughes on the remainder of his California swing. Johnson was incensed. Blaming the old guard Republicans for the continual harassment of the Progressives, Johnson declared that the Republicans had killed Hughes in California. By the time Farnham and Keesling left Long Beach the delicate alliance between Johnson and Hughes had been severed. The Progressive vote was now in question.

The ironic epitaph to the Hughes visit to California was that the race was much closer than anyone had imagined. Though Wall Street continued to bank on Hughes, by early morning after election day it was clear that the Hughes tide had begun to ebb. California became the key state and when it was finally conceded to Wilson, Republicans must have looked in horror at the statistics. The state had been lost by a mere 3775 votes. San Francisco had gone for Wilson by 15,000 votes. Johnson had won on the Progressive ticket by more than 300,000 votes. Southern California may have given Hughes strong support, a plurality of over 40,000 votes, but the former Progressive stronghold of San Francisco had abandoned him.[26]

Undoubtedly the impact of the Hughes luncheon added to the general disenchantment of Californians over Hughes. But, whereas the snub of Johnson was not known to large numbers of people, one must assume that the only voters who felt this was the final straw were those in-the-know, i.e. staunch Progressives. The key to the California disaster is San Francisco. Hughes committed the one unforgivable sin which haunts every politician; he embroiled himself in a local controversy. His attendance at the Commercial Club was obtrusive proof of his enmity to labor. His apparent ties with the Law and Order Committee gave him the odious smell of corruption and ties with Big Business. Though Hughes was later to claim that he had lost the presidency of the United States because he had failed to "shake hands" with the Governor of California, it is far more likely that he kicked away that office as he sat down to dine at the Commercial Club on August 19, 1916.[27]

The Trial of William McDevitt

> *Every anarchist in the United States should be dragnetted by the military, interned by the military, tried and punished by the military.*
>
> ....
>
> *To the top of the pot rises the scum.... To cleanse the pot, to purify the body politic, it should be skimmed off with sure and certain hand.* —San Francisco *Argonaut*, July 7, 1917.[1]

Shortly after the Hughes visit the Committee began to actively solicit the support of another sector of San Francisco public: the clergy. The snub to Archbishop Hanna over the arbitration committee scheme was still fresh in the minds of many San Franciscans and the Committee wished to make certain that this would not affect its image. As a publicity gimmick—and a sop to the clergy—the Committee called a special meeting of the churches of San Francisco to "clear up the Law and Order position."[2]

On August 22, six churches sent representatives to the meeting: Methodist Episcopal Church, First Unitarian Church, First Presbyterian Church, First Baptist Church, Temple Emanu-El and the Central Methodist Church. Representatives from Grace Cathedral and the Protestant Episcopal Church did not attend and sent no explanation for their absence. Hanna was "unable to attend."[3]

The meeting got off to a bad start. Four days previous a group of Methodist ministers had passed a resolution condemning the Law and Order Committee and some of these ministers were present at the meeting.[4] Speaking for these ministers was the Reverend Paul Smith of the Central Methodist Church. Smith had earned a unique reputation in San Francisco by attempting to close down the Barbary Coast, the lower section of town around the docks where prostitution, among other things, prospered. Smith, dressed as a "client," would prowl the Barbary Coast and report the lascivious details to his flock. During his campaign to clean up the city 300 prostitutes marched to his church where they demanded, *en masse* and *in* his church, what was to become of them if prostitution was made illegal. The Reverend Smith had no answer.[5] In regard to labor, Smith was adamant in his opinion that only through collective bargaining could the workers receive "just conditions."[6]

The meeting with the clergy was held at the St. Francis Hotel. The Committee was cordial and came with a resolution prepared for the clergy's endorsement. It read:

> We have held a conference with the Law and Order Committee of the Chamber of Commerce for a broad discussion of the work of that organization. We believe that the position of the Chamber of Commerce will be made clear and that the community knows that there is no attempt to destroy the unions, but that equal justice shall be meted out.[7]

The clergy did not approve the resolution. If they were privy to any special information, as the statement tends to indicate, they were certainly not convinced.

A further snub from the clergy came from the Reverend C.S.S. Dutton of the First Unitarian Church. Dutton, who had been named to the Committee of One Hundred, had made no statement concerning his nomination to that Committee as he had been camping in the Sierra Nevadas at the time. When he returned from his trip he stated that he did not know how he had come to be nominated to such a position or how he was going to resign. With a flair for the dramatic he made the statement to the press from the Republic Cafe, a striker-owned and operated restaurant.[8]

Koster, distraught by both the failure of the meeting with the clergy and Dutton's statement, told the newspapers that Dutton could always resign in the "usual way open to any gentlemen."[9] Furthermore, with the exception of Dutton, Koster claimed that:

> There has not been received by the Chamber of Commerce one single complaint, not one single expression of opposition to the Chamber's policy, and not a single resignation.[10]

This statement, however, was substantially incorrect. Although resignations from the Chamber of Commerce had not yet reached the proportions of the following year (see Appendix III), opposition within the Chamber of Commerce to the Law and Order Committee began to stiffen. The day before Koster made his statement, the Chamber of Commerce saw the budding of internal dissension: 279

members of the Chamber signed a statement opposing the open shop.[11] The solidarity of the Committee was beginning to erode.

On August 25, the same day the 279 members of the Chamber signed the protest, the unions tried to extend their influence into the ecclesiastic community. The general feeling among union men—a dangerous mentality which was beginning to find fertile soil in San Francisco—was that if one did not support the Law and Order Committee, one supported the unions. Representatives of the San Francisco Labor Council, the Waterfront Workers' Federation, the ILA and the teamsters met with 12 members of the San Francisco clergy. These included representatives of the Calvary Methodist–Episcopal Church, First Baptist Church, Methodist Episcopal Church, Calvary Presbyterian Church, Temple Emanu-El, Central Methodist Church, the First Unitarian Church, Grace Cathedral, First Presbyterian Church, Temple Sherith Israel, Hamilton Square Baptist Church and the Protestant Episcopal Church. No member of the Catholic community was present. Hanna was "out of town." The clergy gave the unions as much support as they had given the Law and Order Committee: none.[12]

The ultimate results of both meetings of the clergy was that the churches refused to support either side of the open vs. closed shop campaign. But the most insidious result of the meetings remained that both sides viewed themselves as involved in a battle in which there were no sidelines.

Despite the failure of the Law and Order Committee to achieve the support of the clergy, it did take an aggressive stand against the radicals. One of the most reprehensible acts of the Committee was the trial of William McDevitt *before the Mayor of San Francisco* for the use of inflammatory language at the Anti-Preparedness Day Rally.[13] The legality of this trial is still being debated today.

William McDevitt's notoriety stemmed from the fact that he was a member of the San Francisco Board of Election Commissioners.

Until the Preparedness Day bombing, McDevitt was merely a thorn in the side of the San Francisco community. But with the hysteria created by the outrage, McDevitt became a likely target because of a speech he had made at the Anti-Preparedness Day Rally and his unsavory political affiliations.

The bombing had brought a change to San Francisco. In the wake of the catastrophe the San Francisco press—notably the *Argonaut*—had stepped up their campaign against the radicals in

San Francisco. It was a general contention that the best way for San Francisco to return to "peace and tranquility" was to root out the "hot-bed of anarchy" which San Francisco seemed to have become.[14] The *Argonaut* considered the crusade against the radicals as a blow to unionization since both were the same evil but with different labels.

The *Argonaut* began the drive against McDevitt by calling for an end to the "civic anarchy" which McDevitt seemed to epitomize.[15] Within a few days the Law and Order Committee began to press the mayor to relieve McDevitt of his post. A special committee was formed within the Chamber of Commerce to intensify the pressure on the mayor's office to get McDevitt out of city government. Soon the San Francisco *Call and Post* began demanding the ouster of McDevitt because San Francisco was not in the mood for "jokes or jokers."[16] The *Argonaut* continued the assault:

> It is a crying shame that one capable of such counsel as those embodied in the remarks quoted [from McDevitt's speech] should be permitted to stand upon the official roster of San Francisco.[17]

On August 2, 1916, the special committee of the Chamber of Commerce called upon Mayor Rolph. Included in this group were Howard Nauman, Joseph Durney, George Armes, Marshall Hale and the Chairman, Walter Castle. They submitted to the Mayor what they alleged to be a "copy of the official stenographic report" which had been recorded by an official stenographer present at the Anti-Preparedness Day Rally at Dreamland Rink on July 20.[18] The special committee informed the Mayor that it was a:

> matter of great surprise ... that you have not long ere this dismissed McDevitt from his position as a Cit Official [*sic*].

The crux of their dissatisfaction was:

> We know nothing about his [McDevitt's] efficiency as an election Commissioner — we are not dealing with this proposition. The flexibility of McDevitt's tongue is the question at hand.

The special committee made it clear that they would support the Mayor in not tolerating any "unlawful or anarchistic remarks" in the city.[19]

Rolph suddenly found himself between Scylla and Charybdis. If he bowed to the wishes of the Law and Order Committee and pressed for the removal of McDevitt he would immediately be branded as a cohort of the open shop movement. If he ignored the demand of the Committee and the Chamber of Commerce he would be committing political suicide and appear as a supporter of McDevitt and other radicals in San Francisco. The insinuation could then be drawn that he was a silent proponent of the closed shop. If he did nothing he would lose his credibility as an arbitrator and negotiator whereas in the past his consistent neutral stand had garnered him respect from both camps of the labor–management war. Before he could act, however, McDevitt offered him an honorable out.

The day after the special committee called on the Mayor, Rolph received a letter from McDevitt thanking him for not allowing the Law and Order Committee to "hurry" Rolph into

> any ill-advised action, as at this time all the formalities and decencies of prosecution should be compiled with, especially those who exhibit themselves as the standard and measure of "law and order."

McDevitt stated that he had a "complete and perfect" defense which he would be willing to give in "private or in any open hearing" which Rolph might wish to arrange. McDevitt also expressed the need for some sort of forum to express his position since he felt that the San Francisco press community had been hounding him mercilessly.[20]

Rolph quickly responded. Within 24 hours he wrote McDevitt and included the alleged copy of the speech that had been made on July 20 at the Dreamland Rink. He asked McDevitt to verify the authenticity of the speech and submit a "written statement" at McDevitt's "earliest convenience."[21]

There were only three sections of the speech that were considered inflammatory. The most explosive began with the third line of the speech:

> One of the most heroic men that stands out from and among the nations at the present crisis, one of the very few men that stand out from the warring nations as a real apostle of peace, said not so very long ago, or wrote, in reference to the war, he said: 'If I thought that the men in the trenches would take the only sensible

advice that could be given to them I would say to those soldiers, "Shoot your officers and come home!" That was the advice of Bernard Shaw. And if I thought the people in the Preparedness Parade on Saturday afternoon were in a heroic humor and could take sound advice I might be tempted to say to them 'Shoot in the back of the neck, or somewhere else, in this parade all of the corrupt corporation officials and minions, all of the corrupt bankers, all of the representatives of those powers whose greed is lust for war, shoot them, call it a good day's work and come home.'[22]

The second objectionable portion of the speech dealt with the flag of the United States of America. Although he did not insult the American flag, McDevitt stated his preference for a different flag:

I would prefer for the sake of economy in human life in human ideals, I would prefer that all flags were one. I would favor one color, the color of the heart's blood, to indicate that we stand for life.[23]

This was an unfortunate choice of symbols for many persons associated the red flag with Anarchism.

The final objectionable passage concerned a sniper in Chicago:

A negro prophet the other day in Chicago, heeding the gospel of preparedness, got a rifle and an automatic revolver and some other kinds of weapons which whose use I am not altogether familiar, not being a sportsman, and got his wife to buckle on the armor of defense with plenty of shells and so on, and then began picking off the neighbors, and then was ready for the police force and fought them a form of war on his own account, because he understood he was called upon to prepare in the name of the Lord or someone else, to put out of the way a certain number of people. This is modern war in America.

As the Preparedness Day horror seemed to indicate that a psychopath was responsible, this statement seemed to insinuate that a one-man war was perfectly acceptable since anyone could be called by the "Lord or someone else, to put out of the way a certain number of people."[24]

The rest of the speech was a tirade against the great munitions monopolies and the "gory," "brutal" and "barbaric" attributes of war. It was also gingerly spiced with the catchphrases of Socialism such as the "unification of the working classes" and the "downtrodden." McDevitt had continued the assault on the munitions makers by declaring that there should be no "slaves, no masters, no gun makers, no starving people that will be used for cannons and that sort of thing" if the people of the world—and San Francisco in particular—simply stood up against the war makers. He concluded by stating that the only justification in dying for a country would be to "put into actual practice in our everyday lives those principles sacred in our constitution." The speech was certified by Martin F. Welch, official stenographic reporter of Department Thirteen of the Superior Court of the State of California.[25]

McDevitt's reply to the alleged copy of his speech was caustic. He maintained that the copy of the speech was riddled with errors and inaccuracies probably due to the "prenticehand of one of the assistants" in Welch's office.[26] Significant sections, McDevitt claimed, had been omitted and the reaction of the crowd to the various portions of the speech had not been included. The latter was important because it was indicative of how the speech was received.[27]

To rectify this last shortcoming, McDevitt included a quote from the *Labor Clarion* to indicate that his speech had been meant to be jocular and was accepted as such by the audience:

> Some thousands of people heard Mr. McDevitt speak, and know his paraphrase of Bernard Shaw's advice to the soldiers of Europe was received with laughter by the large audience. Nothing more clearly illustrated the shameful animus of those who have criticised Mr. McDevitt's remarks than that they dare malign a representative American audience such as crowded Dreamland Rink on that evening, by claiming that it would greet with laughter an exhortation to shoot down the leaders of the parade.

McDevitt also urged the Mayor to interpret the speech as a complete unit and not dissect the paragraphs for a single damning sentence. He also urged the Mayor to keep in mind the jocular mood of the audience and how the speech was received. In his defense McDevitt also offered to supply a "specific affidavit to every material statement offered" in his rebuttal. He asked that the Mayor be honest in his case and not submit to the "will of those who wish to have me removed in a cloud of personal slander and political vilification." He warned the Mayor that the Law and Order Committee, the organization responsible for his dilemma, had overestimated its power and was "not representative of the citizens" of San Francisco.[28]

But the pressure on Rolph from the Law and Order Committee and the San Francisco community was enough to force a hearing of some sort. On August 11, Rolph sent a letter to McDevitt:

> You are accused by a Committee of the Chamber of Commerce of having delivered a speech at the Dreamland Rink on the evening of Thursday, July 20, 1916, which it is alleged was inflammatory in character, and calculated to bring about a breach of law and order, and which, it is alleged by said Committee, is a ground for your dismissal from the office which you hold.[29]

The Law and Order Committee, however, was far from satisfied with the handling of the entire affair and filed an injunction against McDevitt on August 14. The *Argonaut* backed the Committee's action and began to insinuate in its columns that a whitewash was underway because the Mayor was "fearful of antagonizing the radical elements which McDevitt is a representative in the municipal administration."[30] A trial was now unavoidable. Rolph informed all parties to be in his chambers for a hearing to commence at 10:00 a.m. on the morning of August 17, 1916.

At the appointed hour all of the interested parties and some spectators met in the Mayor's chambers. Representing the Law and Order Committee were Walter Castle, Marshall Hale, George Armes, Joseph Durney and Howard Nauman. Rolph and McDevitt were present as was Frank M. Drew of the law firm Metson, Drew and McKenzie. Miss B.M. Wilson was sworn in as the official stenographer.[31]

Drew's tactics became immediately clear. He hoped to win the case by linking McDevitt as closely as possible with the IWW, Anarchists and other radical groups in San Francisco. His opening statement began:

> It is the desire of the Chamber of Commerce to present this matter to your Honor so that your Honor may determine whether or not Mr. McDevitt, holding the position of Election Commissioner, in speaking as he has throughout the community, ad-

vertising in the "Blast", after it has said everything that it could possibly say in desecration of the American Flag, advertising to speak at I.W.W. meetings, associating with Anarchists, I.W.W.'s etc. — whether or not in the judgement of your honor Mr. McDevitt should remain an official of the City and County of San Francisco.[32]

McDevitt immediately objected to the introduction of Drew's statement into the record. Claiming that he was being subjected to a guilt by association, McDevitt requested that the opening statement be stricken from the record. Rolph backed McDevitt's objection but left the offending paragraph in the official transcript. (McDevitt actually had little contact with the Anarchists other than advertising in *The Blast*. At one time he had debated with Emma Goldman on the subject "Political Action vs. Direct Action." It should also be noted that when McDevitt accepted the position as election commissioner he had split the Socialist Party in San Francisco because he had chosen a more moderate stand than many of his political cohorts. To join the city administration to many San Francisco Socialists was tantamount to joining the enemy.)[33]

The first witness called was Martin F. Welch, an official reporter for Department Thirteen of the Superior Court of the State of California. He admitted that although he had previously claimed that the speech transcript was a verbatim copy, a careful search of his notes after seeing McDevitt's rebuttal concerning the transcript had uncovered several inconsistencies. When he found the time he was able to more accurately "decipher that portion" of his notes that dealt with the American flag section of the speech, a key point in the trial.[34]

When McDevitt cross-examined Welch he attacked the testimony on two major points. First, he asked Welch if his report had been "official." Welch replied that it was only official inasmuch as it was signed by Welch. Actually, Welch admitted under questioning, he had been hired as a private secretary to record another speech, not McDevitt's. McDevitt insinuated otherwise but Welch denied it.[35]

Then, before he proceeded to his second point, McDevitt entered an objection that he had not been allowed to make an opening statement. Rolph concurred and allowed time for McDevitt's statement but before McDevitt could begin he was forced to postpone the statement in favor of continuing the cross-examination of the witness. According to Drew, Welch was needed for undisclosed duties and would have to finish his testimony at that time.

Continuing the cross-examination McDevitt asked if the report was indeed "true and correct" with the possible exception of the passage concerning the American Flag which had been recently inserted. Welch answered in the affirmative. Then McDevitt began to point out the plethora of slight errors in the transcript. McDevitt, who was a "shorthand writer" himself, had courtroom experience and also had "invented and published a system which [was] not a disconnected vowel system," questioned Welch on specific words in the transcript. McDevitt showed a portion of the transcript where Welch had broken a single sentence into two sentences. In another instance Welch had used the word "accomplish" instead of the word "abolish" which was misleading in the original text since both were "written exactly the same." On another point McDevitt questioned one particular word that had been "misread a pronoun into a conjunction." Consequently the sentence did not make sense. McDevitt was on the verge of forcing Welch to admit that the speech transcript was not actually a verbatim copy when Drew objected to that line of questioning.[36]

McDevitt asked the witness if he had not stated to someone "after the meeting that you did not aim all the way through to take every single word?" Drew objected to the question and stated that the witness was "entitled to [know?] the place where he made it, and the person to whom he said it. He [could not] tell whether he did that unless you [McDevitt] gave him the details." The palaver continued until Rolph instructed the witness to reply. Welch did not recall making such a remark.[37]

McDevitt also remarked that it was poor judgment on Welch's part not to have included the reactions of the audience in the appropriate places. The reactions to the speech, McDevitt claimed, would show the temper of the audience to anyone reading the speech. In a closing philippic—which was actually an opening statement—McDevitt eloquently detailed his case for free speech. He stated that he was a victim of the hysteria of the moment and concluded by stating that he represented "every public official who wishes to have the right to express himself freely on all proper occasions."[38]

Rolph adjourned the meeting but before anyone left the chamber a spectator requested to speak. Rolph allowed it. The spectator stated his name as Paul Scharrenberg, editor of the *Coast Seamen's*

Journal and a member of the Commission on Immigration and Housing. Scharrenberg, referring to Drew specifically and the trial in general, stated that the Law and Order Committee should come to the trial with "clean hands." Then he attempted to introduce Robert Dollar's statement (see page 27), into the record. Drew tried to cut off admission of the statement:

> Mr. Drew. We know what you want to say, but—
> Mr. Scharrenberg. But you don't want me to say it, though.
> Mr. Mayor. Go ahead.

But before Scharrenberg could begin to speak the five members of the Law and Order Committee's special committee demanded that the remark be kept off the record. They claimed that it was irrelevant to the proceeding. The morning session ended with an insinuation by Scharrenberg:

> Mr. Scharrenberg. Gentlemen, I say that I don't think that the Mayor is owned by the Chamber of Commerce as some of you gentlemen think he is.
> Mr. Drew. Can you substantiate that remark, that "some of you gentlemen think he is"? Why do you say that?
> Mr. Scharrenberg. I can substantiate a great many other remarks, too.[39]

McDevitt began the afternoon session by trying to show how ludicrous were the charges that he had incited others to take the law into their own hands. He brought out the fact that the paraders were "notoriously unarmed" and the violence he had referred to was "mere mental shooting." McDevitt also attempted to clarify his position on the red flag. Since he was a Socialist the flag stood for the "brotherhood of man" not the flag of Anarchy which most people associated with the red flag. (McDevitt's attack on the American Flag struck deep at the Committee. To the Committee, the American flag was a symbol of the Law and Order Committee's program — see introductory quote on page 25.) McDevitt's slap at the flag was interpreted by the Committee to be an insulting smear of the United States generally and the Law and Order Committee specifically.[40]

Before he could continue, Durney, one of the members of the special committee of the Law and Order Committee, cut in and complained of the longevity of the hearing. "I think the briefer we can be, the better. We don't come here as prosecutors. We come here as Americans, patriotic Americans, who love and honor the flag." Rolph informed Durney:

> There seems to be an effort to make this hearing as brief as possible. Now we didn't come here for that purpose. We came here for a full hearing on charges against a Commissioner of the City and County of San Francisco.

Drew, responding to Durney's statement, complained that although McDevitt was on trial he objected to the "wandering statements" McDevitt continued to make on "Tolstoi, the former District Attorney writing a history, and the doctrines of anarchism, and flags representing organizations." These subjects had "nothing to do with the case at the bar."[41]

McDevitt defended his verbosity and precise definition of words primarily because this was the crux of his defense. The words he had used in the speech were, in fact, the sole charges against him. Furthermore, to allow the debate on semantics to cease would in effect convict him on the basis of connotative interpretations of his phrases rather than denotative definitions. McDevitt concluded his statement by asking that the charges be dropped. Drew declined to do so and Rolph adjourned the hearing until the next morning.[42]

The second day of McDevitt's hearing began with McDevitt's requesting the right to call witnesses on his behalf. Rolph allowed it and then McDevitt took the stand. Drew asked McDevitt if he had an opening statement. McDevitt replied that he did and began to speak but was immediately cut off by Drew—a tactic that marred the testimony that day. McDevitt did not get another chance to make an opening statement and contented himself to making lengthy, erudite answers to all questions put to him. Together these constituted his statement of position. McDevitt was questioned by the Mayor as to his personal beliefs: Had there been any inflammatory thought in his mind when he delivered the speech? No. Did he believe in the Constitution of the United States and the American Flag? Yes. Was Socialism similar to Anarchism? No. Rolph remarked that although McDevitt claimed to be a Socialist he was accused of making Anarchistic remarks. Drew then attempted to draw McDevitt into stating that a Socialist was liable for what he says just like anyone else. McDevitt agreed, somewhat, but stated:

those who make remarks as Republicans or Democrats are not chargeable with anarchistic remarks, but Socialists are chargeable with such. Republicans and Democrats don't have to defend themselves against such charges.... The ruling parties do not have to do that now.

Rolph gave lukewarm support to McDevitt by backing the right of free speech but sided with Drew in denouncing the right of an Anarchist to be on the Board of Election Commissioners because "Anarchists have no place there."[43]

The rest of the morning and afternoon sessions Drew attempted to draw McDevitt into admitting that he had friends within the radical community. Drew attempted to link McDevitt to Thomas Mooney and Warren Billings then on trial for the Preparedness Day bombing. The high point of the afternoon came when Drew quoted an editorial from *The Blast* from which, he claimed, McDevitt had gotten "his inspiration for the language he used." Then he read the editorial into the record. In part it said:

> There may have been a time when the American flag stood for freedom of conscience and political justice, though even that is doubtful. Today the flag stands only for exploitation and militarism. It is the emblem of prostituted justice and greedy capitalism. It waves proudly over the tents of Ludlow, where women and children of striking miners are burned alive by hired gunmen protected by the American flag. It is the symbol of the subtlest enslavement in the name of democracy and of the most intense exploitation of labor that the world has ever seen. The very fact that men are sent to prison for "desecrating" a rag proves that there is no freedom of conscience under that flag.

Then the trial heated up:

> MR. DREW. We will offer to prove that after that [the editorial from *The Blast*] and continuously up to the last publication of *The Blast*, Mr. McDevitt continues his advertisement, and furthermore, that he has taken subscriptions for *The Blast* up to the time of the last, or perhaps the one before the last.
>
> THE MAYOR. Do you believe that because Mf .McDevitt [sic] advertises in that paper he subscribes to the sentiments of that paper?

MR. DREW. I think, considering what he has said —

THE MAYOR. I want to tell you right now that I advertise in what is known as the Daily Commercial News, but I do not subscribe to the views of that paper. I am diametrically opposed to the views of that paper. And still I advertise in that paper as I am a shipping man.

The argument continued with Drew still trying to draw a conclusion from McDevitt's advertising in *The Blast* and Rolph continuing to disallow it. Eventually Rolph ruled the line of questioning "immaterial, irrelevant and incompetent."[44]

Rolph then changed the topic of conversation and asked the members of the special committee of the Law and Order Committee if any of them had been present at the Anti-Preparedness Day Rally. None of them had been there. Then, asked Rolph, since the copy of the speech was obviously riddled with errors how did they know what had actually been said at the rally? Backing up this question McDevitt offered to bring in depositions to show what had been said.

To this Drew remarked sarcastically that he did not intend to call in all 3800 persons who had been present at the rally as witnesses. Welch was recalled and asked by the Mayor if he had seen "anything or hear[d] anything that [he] would consider an insult to the American flag by Mr. McDevitt?" Welch replied that he had been so busy with Spreckles' speech—the orator before McDevitt—that he had not paid much attention to anything that was being said.[45] (Spreckles of Spreckles' Sugar fame had been notorious with many members of the business community because of his maverick stand on many labor vs. management issues. Although he was a business leader, he not only refused to implement the open shop in his factory but fought it vigorously on the unions' behalf. The *Argonaut* called him, among other titles, a "master of anarchy."[46])

Under cross examination Welch admitted that he had not transcribed the speech immediately but had done so at the request of the Law and Order Committee *after* the Preparedness Day bombing. And, Welch continued, he had assumed that the meeting was a Socialist meeting because one of the ushers had a badge that read "Youn People's Socialist League or something like that." McDevitt gave the Mayor a list of the speakers, which included many prominent members of the San Francisco labor and religious community. There was even a rabbi present. Welch still maintained that he believed it had been a Socialist meeting.[47]

McDevitt then began introducing his witnesses. One was the past Grand President of the Native Sons of the Golden West, another was a United States marshal, another was the United States Immigration Commissioner and yet another was a representative of the San Francisco Center—the forerunner of the San Francisco League of Women Voters. Ten witnesses were called by McDevitt and several spectators were allowed to introduce their own testimony. The witnesses represented a wide variety of occupations and political beliefs but all maintained that the speech had not been inflammatory. Rolph adjourned the session for the day but left Thursday, August 21, open for a final session.[48]

On the final day of McDevitt's trial Drew recalled McDevitt to the stand. Then, following the same line of questioning he had begun on the first day of the trial, Drew began questioning McDevitt on an article he had allegedly written in *The Revolt* in 1911. When Rolph questioned the validity—and legitimacy—of introducing evidence that was five year old, Drew replied that San Francisco had a right to know "the kind of shadow a man casts in his walk through the community." Furthermore, it was the responsibility of the Law and Order Committee to "show the kind of shadow" McDevitt cast. Rolph was unimpressed and refused to accept the article as evidence. He asked Drew if he had any witnesses to call. Drew replied in the negative. Rolph then adjourned the hearing and stated that a decision would be submitted to both parties. Thus ended the trial of William McDevitt.[49]

In the final analysis the trial was a travesty. The only charge was the use of inflammatory language that may or may not have sparked the Preparedness Day bombing. Since it has been generally assumed that neither Mooney nor Billings was guilty, this point cannot be proven one way or the other. The bulk of the prosecution, however, was not in trying to establish that McDevitt used inflammatory language but that he was associated with the radical community in San Francisco. Then, it can be assumed, McDevitt could be found guilty of incitement to bomb.

Rolph, on the other hand, was careful to maintain his position as a neutral and would not be rushed to judgment. He undoubtedly found the trial distasteful but necessary for appearances. It is, needless to say, highly irregular for a "trial" with all of the trappings of a case at bar to be held before a civil official rather than a judicial figure. Yet it was conducted as a trial with a prosecutor and many of the formalities.

80 Committee of Vigilance

Although it was called a trial, the procedure was open enough to allow it to become a laughing stock; there was no opening statement allowed the defense, witnesses were allowed to leave because of other duties; and a constant stream of spectators put their testimony into the record. Many questioned the validity of the trial.

Overall the trial reflected three points of view which existed not only in the Mayor's chamber but within the San Francisco community as well. On one hand was Drew who kept trying to link McDevitt to the Anarchists. And McDevitt, trying to become a martyr, continued to exert himself as such as he filled the transcript with his politics and piety. Rolph, sitting on the sidelines of the carnival, was the participant who kept in mind that there was a case of free speech involved and a rational, legal and equitable decision had to be made no matter how the clowns performed. McDevitt's speech may have been indiscrete, but it was not inflammatory.

The central issue at the trial was not McDevitt's fate but rather the attempt by the Law and Order Committee to extend its influence into the general community by appearing as a watchdog over the more disreputable elements in San Francisco. It was undoubtedly hoped that Mayor Rolph would find himself forced to join with the Committee. The McDevitt trial seemed to appropriate lever. But in reality the trial showed the Law and Order Committee that it was much weaker than it had presumed it was. Mayor Rolph could not be cajoled or threatened away from his neutral position. Though history does not record the exact words, McDevitt was exonerated and he held his position as an Election Board member for years after the trial. For the Law and Order Committee, the trial was a miserable failure as well as an embarrassment. But infinitely more important, it was the trial of William McDevitt which has established the Law and Order Committee firmly in the annals of vigilantism.

The Committee vs. the Unions

> ...every contract, combination in the form of trust or otherwise, or conspiracy, in restraint of trade or commerce among the several states or with foreign nations [is illegal]. — Sherman Anti-Trust Act, 1890.

With the collapse of the Lumberyard strike on July 25, the Law and Order Committee began to work on long range plans for the city-wide open shop. Being in an isolated region as far as available manpower was concerned, the Committee foresaw an advantage that could be exploited. In anticipation of city-wide lockouts to impose the open shop, it became essential to have enough strikebreakers immediately available to fill the places of the striking union men. If the Committee could fill the place of every striker the lockout would be a success. If the Committee could succeed it would be the first time in more than three decades that the entire city had been exclusively open shop. But, if the Committee failed to win decisively, it could mean economic chaos for the city. Many businessmen were aware of this possibility and for that reason were hesitant to join in any city-wide open shop campaign.

In response to the manpower question the Committee formed the American Stevedore Company, an organization created to be a monopoly of nonunion labor.[1] With this instant supply of nonunion labor any lockout would be guaranteed enough manpower to survive. Whereas in the past the San Francisco employers had been forced to send to other cities for this manpower, now it was available within the city limits.

On August 23, the Committee had its first chance to use the American Stevedore Company. For the second time in 1916 the Lumberyards went back on strike. Immediately the 38 members of the Retail Lumber Dealers Association announced that they intended to operate their establishments as open shops.[2] They locked out their striking workmen and began hiring strikebreakers from the American Stevedore Company. There was little violence but the strike brought to play a new twist — a cache of dynamite discovered at the Hartwood Lumber Company.[3] The Hartwood Company had

81

been in the limelight for the previous few days because it had recruited the aid of the Law and Order Committee in order to bring suit against its striking workmen. It was generally assumed that radical elements within the unions were responsible. Searches of other lumberyards revealed another bundle of dynamite sticks, these ready to be exploded, at the James Hardy Lumber Company, the only lumberyard to sign with the unions for the closed shop.[4] Speculation on this find was lacking and no arrests were made but it did add a touch of the macabre to the strike. Earlier in the year there had been a million dollar fire on the docks and though it was probably not strike-related, *The Blast* prophetically announced that more violence was yet to come:

> Repeated visitations of the "red cock" will impress the masters with the novel idea that strikers are "on the job" even if they have quit working.[5]

Statements such as this did little to allay the fears of the struck businessmen or the striking unions.

The discovery of the dynamite heightened the suspicions of both the unions and the employers. It reinforced the opinion among businessmen that the unions were bent on violence. The finding of the second cache seemed to reinforce union fears that a cabal within the business community was so set on destroying the unions that they were willing to stoop to violence to achieve that end. The already polarized situation was exacerbated with the paranoidal allegations of each side fulfilled.

One of the most vociferous strikes, however, was the combined Structural Steel and Architectural Iron Workers strike. Before it was finally resolved the Mayor, the Committee and the unions were locked in what the newspapers dubbed a "state of war."[6]

The structural steel workers had been pressing for an eight-hour day for several months and finally informed their employers that they wanted the change from the nine-hour to eight-hour day implemented no later than July 10, 1916. Fifty-four of the 64 San Francisco firms quickly agreed to the change but the ten leading firms in San Francisco refused. The ten firms—Dyer Brothers, Mortenson Construction Company, Pacific Rolling Mill Company, Ralston Iron Works, Schrader Iron Works, Western Iron Works, Central Iron Works, Vulcan Iron Works, Withington Iron Works and the Pacific Structural Company—were adamant over the demands because of the costs involved. The ten firms even offered to open their books for public scrutiny to show that such a change would not be financially feasible. And, since these ten firms controlled over 90 percent of the industry's production, their refusal placed the entire strike in jeopardy.[7]

Rather than face the unions individually, these ten firms agreed to stand together. Forming an organization known as the Building Trades Employers Association they would be able to maintain the solidarity necessary to weather a prolonged confrontation. Each firm pledged a bond, ranging from $1500 to $10,000, as a guarantee of cooperation.[8] In this monolithic confederation the ten firms felt they could successfully negotiate and/or lockout as a unit.

On July 25 the ten firms — with the support of the Law and Order Committee — announced that they intended to resume operations immediately. Through Grant Fee, president of the Building Trades Employers Association and within 48 hours a member of the Committee of One Hundred, the companies demanded that all workers return to their jobs by July 28 or the ten firms would install an open shop.[9] Since there was not enough time for the unions to respond, the ten firms began operating on a nine-hour, open shop basis.

The Committee had been waiting for just such an opportunity. This coalition of the steel firms and the Law and Order Committee would be the epitome of a symbiotic relationship. The firms needed the manpower and financial assistance to survive the strike. The Committee needed a proving ground to test its strength in a face-to-face confrontation with the unions. Immediately after they had declared for an open shop the ten firms began receiving nonunion labor from the American Stevedore Company, courtesy of the Law and Order Committee.[10] The Committee was also liberal in the supplying of armed guards to protect those strikebreakers as well as with financial assistance to keep the firms solvent.

The struggle continued for many months with both sides believing they were on the verge of success. The ten firms attempted to prolong the strike as long as possible in order to bankrupt the unions and force them to return to work. The unions, on the other hand, felt that if the fabricating mills were forced to use nonunion labor long enough, the companies would have no choice but to give in to the eight-hour day. (Though the strikebreakers were available and cheap, they were unskilled. Thus the firms were getting scabs to do the work but the quality of that work tended to be inferior.)

The unions' reasoning proved to be the more realistic. On August 16, the Pacific Rolling Mill Company sent a letter to Mayor Rolph stating that although it still supported the open shop and the nine-hour day most of the nonunion labor provided by the Committee was

> unfamiliar with fabrication of structural steel and while they are adapting themselves as rapidly as can be expected it is essential that we proceed with our work in a cautious manner due to the absolute accuracy which is necessary.[11]

Suddenly, in mid-August, the monolithic front of the Building Trades Employers Association was broken when the Vulcan Iron Works bolted and signed with the unions. Shortly thereafter three more firms — Central Iron Works, Withington Iron Works and the Pacific Rolling Mill Company — also capitulated. (One of these firms did not finally sign with the unions until a boycott had been declared against it.)

Later these four firms claimed that they had been forced to join the structural steel coalition under threats that

> arrangements had been made with railroads, banks and other companies so that any employer who did not join the organization [Building Trades Employers Association] would find his materials were sidetracked, delayed and missent: banks would call his loans, and he would be driven out of business.[12]

Furthermore, they claimed that they had agreed to join the coalition with the understanding that the lockout was only to be for 30 days so that the eight-hour day would not be given too readily. It was also their contention that the bargaining body of the coalition "refused to confer at all with the strikers."[13]

Although these four firms had signed with the unions, their troubles were not yet over. The six remaining firms immediately sued for the bonds which had been posted as a guarantee of solidarity. The litigation over this issue was to continue for years.

To add further pressures to the six recalcitrant firms, the unions began a product boycott. Backed by the California Building Trades Council, the boycott was aimed at defeating the Building Trades Employers Association and the Law and Order Committee at their own game. A circular was sent out which stated

LAW AND ORDER!

To the Citizens of San Francisco:

THERE HAS SUDDENLY ARISEN A SITUATION IN THIS CITY DEMANDING THE ATTENTION OF EVERY THOUGHTFUL, LOYAL AND PATRIOTIC SAN FRANCISCAN.

The Building Trades Council of San Francisco has declared a boycott upon seven structural steel firms, which at this time are exercising the right granted to every American citizen of liberty of action by employing working men without accepting dictation from any source whatsoever as to whom they should employ.

The announcement of the boycott against these firms was made in a circular letter sent by the Building Trades Council to the architects of San Francisco.

This letter is signed by O. A. Tveitmoe, Secretary of the Building Trades Council of San Francisco. The letter includes a list of firms classed as "fair" and a list classed as "unfair."

THE LAW AND ORDER COMMITTEE of the SAN FRANCISCO CHAMBER OF COMMERCE does not publish these names here because this Committee will not be a party to the circulation of a boycott. This letter is as follows:

"BUILDING TRADES COUNCIL OF SAN FRANCISCO
"BUILDING TRADES TEMPLE
"San Francisco, Cal., September 28, 1916.
"Please be advised that the following ornamental iron and structural steel firms are employing union mechanics and helpers, and operating their shops on the basis of an eight-hour workday: * * *
"In order that honest and fair dealings may obtain, we beg to inform you that the following seven unfair firms employ non-union workers, and operate their shops on the basis of a nine-hour workday: * * *
"Union men affiliated with the Building Trades Council of San Francisco and the State Building Trades Council of California will refuse to handle or place any material fabricated by any of the seven unfair firms hereinbefore mentioned, and they will not work on jobs where said non-union, nine-hour manufactured material is used.   "Very respectfully,   (Signed)   O. A. TVEITMOE,
"Secretary Building Trades Council of San Francisco."

THIS PLAINLY MEANS THAT THE BUILDING TRADES UNIONS OF THIS CITY AND STATE INTEND, by threat of strike and boycott, to prevent seven business houses of this city from having business intercourse with their fellow-citizens until they agree to conduct their business in accordance with the demands of a powerful combination in the community.

These seven structural steel firms fabricate 90% or more of the structural steel fabricated in San Francisco.

This boycott is directed solely against these San Francisco firms, whereas structural steel fabricated in any other part of the United States, regardless of the conditions under which it is fabricated, under longer hours, lower wages, and non-union conditions, is accepted here with no restrictions whatever.

THE LAW AND ORDER COMMITTEE of the SAN FRANCISCO CHAMBER OF COMMERCE will not now (nor has it at any time in the past) enter into any question of hours and wages between employer and employee. The LAW AND ORDER COMMITTEE stands exactly where it stood when it was organized on July 10, 1916. This Committee was formed to execute the permanent policy of the SAN FRANCISCO CHAMBER OF COMMERCE. That policy demands:

1. *The integrity of contractual relations.*
2. *The maintenance of Law and Order.*
3. *The policy of the Open Shop, insisting upon the right to employ union or non-union workers, in whole or in part, as the parties involved may elect.*

THIS COMMITTEE TAKES THE POSITION THAT THE BOYCOTT IS UNAMERICAN. This Committee concurs thoroughly with the decision of the Federal Anthracite Coal Strike Commission, which, in its report to President Theodore Roosevelt, on the anthracite coal strike, said:

"It (the boycott) is an attempt of many, by concerted action, to work their will upon another who has exercised his legal right to differ with them in opinion and in conduct. It is tyranny, pure and simple, and as such is hateful, no matter whether attempted to be exercised by few or by many, by operators or by workmen, and no society that tolerates or condones it can justly call itself free."

THIS COMMITTEE indorses this further expression in the report of the Anthracite Coal Strike Commission:

"The right thus to work can not be made to depend upon the approval or disapproval of the personal character and conduct of those who claim to exercise this right. If this were otherwise, then those who remain at work might, if they were in the majority, have both the right and power to prevent others, who choose to cease to work, from so doing.
"This all seems too plain for argument. Common sense and common law alike denounce the conduct of those who interfere with this fundamental right of the citizen. The assertion of the right seems trite and commonplace, but that land is blessed where the maxims of liberty are commonplace."

IN CONNECTION WITH THE RIGHT TO WORK, this Committee further indorses the judgment rendered by the Honorable Joseph Fitch of New York, who, on September 21st of this year, in sentencing a defendant arrested during the car strike cases, said:

"The laws of this country are very severe against capitalists who combine to raise the price of products or anything of that kind. The laboring man can still combine, if he wants, with his fellows, to strike or quit work. That is a necessary instrument for his protection in his hands. But if there are a thousand car conductors in Queens County, and nine hundred and ninety-nine of them decide to go on a strike, and there is one man of them that wants to work, and who declines to go on strike with the nine hundred and ninety-nine, I hold, and if I were Mayor of New York I should hold, if it brought down the City Hall upon my head, that the whole force of the police of the entire City of New York, if it were necessary, should protect that one man against the nine hundred and ninety-nine, and he should drive a car if he were the only man in Queens that wanted to do it and his Company were willing to employ him. Now, that would be my attitude, because that is the old American idea of freedom, and we are getting pretty far away from it now in many respects."

But, in face of these expressions of broad Americanism from sources of integrity and soundness, the community of San Francisco is confronted with this boycott.

MR. ARCHITECT, what are YOU going to do about this boycott?

MR. OWNER, what are YOU going to do about this boycott?

MR. CITIZEN, what are YOU going to do about this boycott?

THE LAW AND ORDER COMMITTEE
Of the San Francisco Chamber of Commerce

A page from the Argonaut, October 14, 1916.

> Union men affiliated with the Building Trades Council of California will refuse to handle or place any material fabricated by any of the seven* unfair firms hereinbefore mentioned, and they will not work on jobs where said nonunion, nine-hour manufacturing is used.[14]

The boycott was a calculated risk. Dollar for dollar the unions could not defeat the Committee and the Building Trades Employers Association. If the boycott was successful there was always the possibility that an injunction might be issued. If the boycott was unsuccessful the unions would have demonstrated their own weakness and the structural steel strike would collapse.

The Committee immediately began to counteract the circular by beginning a publicity campaign of its own. Huge advertisements in most of the city's newspapers stated that "THERE HAS SUDDENLY ARISEN A SITUATION IN THIS CITY DEMANDING THE ATTENTION OF EVERY THOUGHTFUL AND PATRIOTIC SAN FRANCISCAN."[15] The advertisements lamented the fact that the unions could not see the position of business and felt compelled to take their "unAmerican" stand. Furthermore, the firms were well within their rights by

> exercising the right granted to every American citizen of liberty of action by employing working men without accepting dictation from any source whatsoever as to whom they should employ.[16]

Eventually Mayor Rolph became involved in the strike. Since the beginning of the strike his position had been to maintain a neutral position. In the midst of the violence and the bombing hysteria Rolph was the unofficial arbitrator in constant communication with the various striking unions and their respective employers. He had held several meetings with the structural steel unions and the six remaining firms, climaxing in an explosive meeting on November 10.

After listening to both sides of the controversy, Rolph suggested, as a possible compromise, that the six remaining firms try the eight-hour day for "six or nine months."[17] After that time, if the San Francisco steel industry could not compete successfully with other steel fabricating plants elsewhere in the United States, "another conference could be arranged."[18]

*One of the seven firms bolted immediately after this circular.

From the firms' point of view there were two basic flaws to this proposal. Other than the fact that they did not feel ready to settle yet, the Mayor's proposal offered to establish an eight-hour day on a trial basis. But once established the eight-hour day would be more difficult to extirpate. Even if the firms agreed to such a condition, there were fears that this might give the unions and the Mayor the inclination to believe that the firms were weakening in their resolve. Secondly, the Mayor's proposal stated that another conference "could be arranged," not that another conference "would be arranged." Often a single letter can change the entire complexion of an agreement. (It is also interesting to note that on September 2, 1916, Woodrow Wilson had signed the Adamson Act into effect making the eight-hour day Federal policy. The structural steel demand for the same consideration was well timed—whether this was by accident or well planned is a matter of conjecture.)

Four days later the six companies sent an outraged letter to the Mayor claiming that he had "taken an unfair stand" against them by forcing them to do "a thing that in [their] opinion [would] act as the last straw in the ruination" of the structural steel industry in San Francisco. Furthermore, five reasons were listed to back their refusal to implement the eight-hour day:

> (1) No other city in the United States had a structural steel industry running on an eight-hour day,
>
> (2) San Francisco was already paying a wage that was 35% higher than in any structural steel industry in the United States,
>
> (3) There was no difference in "freight rates between raw and fabricated materials" from the East Coast to San Francisco, which reduced profits,
>
> (4) There was a total loss of waste materials which could be disposed of by non-San Francisco firms "to good advantage" and
>
> (5) There was a difference in shop rules between the East Coast and the San Francisco mills.

On November 17, the structural steel union responded. Writing for the unions, William Michel, Secretary of the Housesmiths and Architectural Iron Works Local 78, attempted to show, point by point, how unrealistic the stand of the companies was:

> (1) For the past decade the eight-hour day had been tried in the structural steel industry and had proved successful;

(2) East Coast firms not only paid as high a wage as San Francisco firms, but in many cases a higher wage;

(3) Competition with East Coast firms was minimal since no East Coast firm had won a contract for a job in San Francisco for several years thus making freight rates moot and

(4) Waste was not a bone of contention since the scraps from large jobs were used on smaller jobs or sold to other companies.[20]

The contentions of both parties, however, are suspect. As neither the unions nor the employers bothered to mention any particular steel industry in the United States—other than "East Coast firms"—it would be impossible to compare San Francisco statistics with other structural steel industries. Although it is conceivable than an East Coast firm might build a structure in San Francisco, it does not seem logical that the firm would transport its own materials by "freight" from the East Coast. It is also a matter of logic to sell the scraps of a large job rather than just throw them out. It would seem that a competent businessman would naturally want to make the most profit out of his efforts, using even the leftovers.

Furthermore, in regard to an eight-hour day, Michel quoted Mr. R. Slavin, superintendent of the Judson Manufacturing Company, who stated that, in regard to the eight-hour day, production

> will be increased fourteen percent, and that overhead expenses, cost of oil, lighting, etc. will be reduced, The men are far more efficient, more willing, more capable of first class work under the new system. Directly in charge of the work here as I am, I have been in a position to closely observe the new order, and I can safely make this unqualified statement, "a worker can and will do more in eight hours than in twelve" [sic].

Michel also quoted Mr. Mortenson, proprietor of the Mortenson Iron Works, on the recalcitrant firms:

> We [the six remaining open shop firms] believe that the eight hour day can be granted at present, but when the war is over what are we going to do?[22]

One of the gnawing facts of economic life has been that war is usually good for business because it stimulated demand. With the First World War on the horizon it was to be expected that there would be an increased demand for machinery of war. This in turn would stimulate the steel industry throughout the United States. Mortenson, however, was looking beyond the war and making a judgment which had little basis in fact.

In spite of the conferences, negotiations and boycott, the unions and the six firms could not come to an agreement. Supported by the Law and Order Committee, the firms continued to hold out for the nine-hour day. It seemed that nothing could stop the Law and Order open shop juggernaut.

But the capitulation of the four mills to the unions should have been an indication to the Committee that all was not going well with the open shop campaign. With the mounting costs of the strikes and the violence which accompanied them, the price tag on a city-wide open shop was becoming prohibitive. Many businessmen were beginning to look at the open shop with a much more critical eye. The business community could only be coerced so far and by mid-November many businessmen no longer held the open shop in such high esteem. In the final analysis it would be the businessman who was the loser. After a strike a striker could find another job; a businessman might have lost years of investments. And, as the open shop campaign spread, there was an uneasy feeling in the business community that they were the sacrificial lamb for a cabal of Big Business interests represented by the Law and Order Committee.

Though many businesses were turning cool toward the open shop campaign in November, in August the Committee was still riding the crest of one of the greatest waves of popularity in San Francisco history. Though the Committee had the finances to run the open shop campaign indefinitely, it was still sensitive to the accusation that it represented not the smaller businessmen but Big Business.

To counteract this charge, the Committee decided to inflate its credibility by recruiting more of the smaller city businesses to its fold. What was needed was not financial support but widespread popular backing. The Chamber of Commerce *Activities* made this clear when it printed that what was needed was the

> moral backing of the entire San Francisco business community in order to carry on the work successfully; the financial backing for these undertakings [open shop] will undoubtedly be taken care of, but the active, individual and collective support and assistance of the businessmen of the city is needed in this work.[23]

To this end the Committee hired H. Van Rensselaer Chase, an experienced public relations manager. He was hired on July 26 and given a goal of five thousand new members. It was not until August 17, that Chase was able to start the campaign.[24]

Twelve thousand personal invitations to join the Chamber were sent out to the business community. Announcements were placed in the papers and personal appeals were made by members of the Chamber. The invitations were actually a thinly veiled request for support in the open shop campaign. They included the usual phraseology of the necessity to "pull together for the common good" and "become identified with this work," but the invitations negated the entire concept which the Chamber had followed in the past; the invitations insinuated involvement. A cryptic passage near the end of the invitation stated:

> The Chamber will not hesitate to attack any problem in the interest of the whole community, no matter how difficult it may be or what may be the osbtacle in the path of its execution.[26]

Many businessmen saw through the veneer, including Mayor Rolph. On his copy of the invitation Rolph penciled in "What about organized labor?"[26]

The campaign was scheduled to last four days: August 30, 31, September 1 and 2. It was quite successful. At the start of the campaign the Chamber of Commerce had numbered only 2474. By the end of the campaign the San Francisco Chamber of Commerce had netted an additional 4808 members bringing the total membership to 7282. This was an increase of almost 300 percent. Besides adding an estimated quarter-million dollars to the open shop coffers it dramatically demonstrated that the Chamber of Commerce and the Law and Order Committee did have the backing of the San Francisco business community. On September 9, 1916, when the new members were officially entered on the role of the San Francisco Chamber of Commerce, the total membership for the Chamber was 7940. This made the San Francisco Chamber the largest in the United States.[27]

But there was still antagonism to the Law and Order Committee, most notably in the figure of Mayor Rolph. To the Committee, Rolph was a question mark. While it could not be said that he was a staunch supporter of the Law and Order Committee, neither was he a sympathetic friend of labor. Rolph, being a businessman, was financially more inclined to the business community but as the Mayor of San Francisco he tried to represent all the people, business and labor alike. But in spite of the fact that he was in a formidable position in the city administration he did little to oppose the Committee other than to launch an occasional verbal barrage. The first — and last — face-to-face confrontation between the Mayor and the Committee was in November over the construction of the tubercular wing of the San Francisco Hospital.[28]

The bid for the construction of the tubercular wing had been won earlier in the year by Dyer Brothers, one of the hold-out structural steel firms. Work had begun with disgruntled architectural iron workers who sympathized with the structural steel strike. A confrontation soon developed when Dyer Brothers neglected to put up planking for the protection of the workmen on the ground. This planking was essential to keep any falling tools or building materials from striking a workman on the ground.[29]

An Industrial Accident Commission inspector informed Dyer Brothers of this negligence but Dyer Brothers refused to rectify the matter. When the planking was not installed, the architectural iron workers walked off their jobs in mid-November.[30]

Rolph, again acting as moderator, scheduled a meeting between the striking unions and the company. Acting as a catalyst Rolph was able to make substantial progress in negotiations when the Law and Order Committee pressured Dyer Brothers to break off negotiations and declare the hospital, like their structural steel plant, an open shop. Again the Committee guaranteed financial support, nonunion labor and armed guards. Whether Dyer Brothers wished to do so or not, it was hopelessly indebted to the Committee and had no choice but to acquiesce. If Dyer Brothers had refused, the Committee could have withdrawn its strikebreakers and armed guards from the structural steel mill and Dyer Brothers would have been forced to capitulate to the unions. Dyer Brothers was inextricably tied to the Law and Order Committee. The *Labor Clarion* described the situation with a venomous pen:

> It seems that both parties [of the architectural iron workers' dispute] appreciated the merits of the Mayor's position [to act as a mediator] and were about to agree, when that band of buzzards known as the Law and Order Committee of the Chamber of Commerce, creatures without hearts or souls, sympathies or emotions and moved only by the instincts of gluttonous greed,

stepped in and prevented an adjustment, with a desire to inconvenience organized labor.[31]

To further complicate the hospital confrontation, the Law and Order Committee had hired former police chief George Wittman to oversee its armed guards. Now not only did Wittman carry the obvious stigma of being a hireling of the Law and Order Committee, he also bore the albatross of corruption as he had been forced to resign from the Police Department of San Francisco under charges of graft. The Law and Order Committee could have chosen a better representative of "law and order" as the head of its security force.[32]

The Committee also entered a dispute over the construction of another hospital, the hospital at the University of California at San Francisco. Construction of this hospital had begun with men who were "alleged to be plasterers" but were actually strikebreakers furnished by the Law and Order Committee.[33] These workmen did such a poor job that when the Regents of the University of California met, they decided to cancel the contract and hire another firm to complete the plastering. The old crew and their guards, however, refused to leave the building site and the San Francisco police had to arrest the strikebreakers before the work could begin again.

The solution to the construction of the tubercular wing of the San Francisco Hospital was not as simple as just terminating a contract. F.A. Reardon, president of the San Francisco Public Works Department, the city agency responsible for the construction of the San Francisco Hospital, ordered all armed guards off the hospital premises. He was backed by Mayor Rolph. When Rolph was asked how he would handle the situation if the armed guards refused to leave, he answered, "Arrest them if they don't get off the property."[34]

When the police arrived at the hospital they found that the ar-armed guards had moved to an adjacent street. This may have been a clever way of avoiding arrest but it did not guarantee the safety of the strikebreakers who promptly "quit their jobs and disappeared." Dyer Brothers was then given three days to complete the job.[35] As this was a physical impossibility Rolph was allowed to cancel the contract and to order Reardon to let the San Francisco Board of Public Works finish the building. Speaking for the City and County of San Francisco Rolph stated:

> I am through with whimsical and technical quibblings over this hospital job, and it will be finished by the city itself and the

cost deducted from the money covered by the Dyer Brothers' contract. The Law and Order Committee of the Chamber of Commerce is financing Dyer Brothers as a part of the open shop campaign, but they shall not be permitted to bring suffering and death upon helpless human beings in order to satisfy their vicious desires.[36]

With the arrival of the Mayor and the full weight of the city administration behind him, the Law and Order Committee was forced to admit defeat. Even with the backing of the general public and a tremendous budget, the Committee could not hope to defeat the power of city hall. Withdrawing its support from the six remaining steel firms caused those firms to go down to a humiliating defeat. By January, 1917, the six companies had signed with the unions for an eight-hour day.

At the height of the confrontation between Dyer Brothers and the Architectural Iron Workers Union, national elections were held. Although the major issue was the presidential race between Hughes and Wilson, of equal importance to labor were two ordinances on the San Francisco ballot, numbers 8 and 9. Ordinance 8 would prohibit all speeches in the streets without a permit. Ordinance 9, a far more restrictive proposal, would prohibit all picketing within the city limits. "Picketing," as defined by the ordinance, was any "loud or unusual tones of speech ... the carrying of or display of a banner ... or any loud or unusual noise."[37] These legal perimeters were so broad that virtually anything could be considered picketing. The unions were well aware of the fact that if the antipicketing ordinance passed it would literally take the guts out of every strike within the city limits. This appeared to be the ultimate weapon in the Committee's arsenal.

For several months prior to the election the ordinances had been key issues in the open shop campaign. Through the use of a massive public relations campaign, a device the Law and Order Committee was becoming adept at using, the Committee attempted to associate the prestige of the Chamber of Commerce and the Law and Order Committee with the passage of the ordinances. In a special antipicketing drive the Committee had gathered 26,434 signatures to place the ordinance on the ballot.[38] Then advertisements were placed in most newspapers sold in San Francisco—neglecting, of course, the union presses—and slide shows in movie houses brought the message to San Franciscans. The Chamber of Commerce also gave the newspapers many chances to quote prominent members of that body on picketing. Allan G. Wright, an attorney for the Chamber, was quoted as saying that "'Peaceful picketing' is a contradiction in terms." Koster, quoted with glee in the *Argonaut*, was reported to have said that "picketing is impractical in connection with industrial peace and public picketing is a scandal."[39] As a last minute effort the Committee and the Chamber hired 400 telephone operators to work two shifts a day on 175 telephones to urge the public to get out and vote in favor of the passage of the ordinances.[40]

The results of the election were contradictory. Though Ordinance 9 passed it did so by a mere 6 percent. Ordinance 8 also passed but only 50 percent of the issues favored by the Chamber and the Committee in the Chamber of Commerce *Activities* were approved by the voters. Thanks to the myopic politics of the Committee, Charles Evans Hughes was narrowly defeated. But the election results carried a message to the Committee. Though many members of the San Francisco community trusted its advice in labor matters, as seen by the passage of the two ordinances, the Committee's peripheral influence was lacking. In labor matters it may have been considered knowledgeable but in matters which did not relate to the industrial conditions of San Francisco the Committee was not considered by many to represent the views of all San Franciscans. The elections should have driven home the message that the power of the Committee was on the wane.

The election, as prophetic as it may have been, proved disastrous to the Culinary strike. On November 7, 1916, picketing within the city limits became illegal. Although there was some grumbling about taking the vote to court no action was taken by the unions and with no pickets the strike folded within a few short weeks. The collapse of the Culinary strike was a devastating blow to the culinary unions. The citizens of San Francisco had killed the strike by their vote, union membership had dropped by more than 60 percent and an industry-wide open shop appeared to exist throughout the city.[41]

For the Committee the victory was pyrrhic. In spite of the fact that it had triumphed the Committee had spent over 50 percent of its total budget for the victory. Though open shop plaques had disappeared from the windows of the restaurants and cafeterias, most employers preferred to hire skilled union labor rather than the stopgap strikebreakers provided through the American Stevedore Company. Though an insignificant number of strikebreakers were eventually hired in the culinary industry, the employers had been rehiring embittered strikers throughout the strike and with the collapse of the strike many strikers took back jobs they had left to join the strike.[42]

But the most significant message to be sent by the people of San Francisco was that the power of labor in San Francisco was truly moribund. The passage of the two ordinances indicated that the city was tired of the violence which had rocked the streets since early June of 1916. The waterfront strikes, the lumberyard violence, a bombing and finally a vicious restaurant workers' strike which brought violence into downtown San Francisco had been more than many San Franciscans could stomach. During the three months of the Culinary strike there had been 27 incidents of arrests, threats, beatings, property damage, throwing of food and stinkbombs and "filthy tactics."[43] To San Franciscans it was just more violence and when they had a chance to express their dissatisfaction, they were willing to eliminate the violence at the expense of the labor unions' right to picket.

"The End of the Trail"

In December of 1916 the Committee finished its work for the year with the publication of a pamphlet chronicling for posterity its activities since inception. Sandwiched between glossy pictures and elaborate engravings, the Committee listed the strikes it had entered and the details of the Preparedness Day bombing—a rather significant pairing. Listed in detail were all of the incidents of violence in the Waterfront strikes, Lumberyard strikes, Structural Steel boycott and strike, Culinary strike and the violence precipitated by each action. Also included was a section on the passage of the two ordinances which killed the Culinary strike. In a conscious attempt to link the union troubles with the Preparedness Day bombing, two full front page sheets from the San Francisco *Chronicle* and the San Francisco *Examiner* reporting in grotesque detail the extent of the damage, and listings of the dead and maimed were included in foldouts within the pamphlet. Mayor Rolph and Archbishop Hanna were not mentioned and Robert Dollar's statement concerning the sending of strikers to the hospital was noticeably lacking. McDevitt's trial before the Mayor was also missing. Through the courtesy of the San Francisco Chamber of Commerce these pamphlets were sent to other Chambers of Commerce and libraries throughout the country.[1]

The pamphlet was nothing short of an attempt to link the unions with the violence in the streets of San Francisco and the Preparedness Day outrage. Although it may be said that the violence resulting from a strike was undoubtedly union related, it would be undeniably false to state that the unions, in any way, were responsible for the Preparedness Day bombing. Though there may have been some doubt in the minds of San Franciscans, even after the publication of two monumental works, to other Americans in other cities across the United States, who happened to peruse the pamphlets, the implication was clear: the unions were to blame for the Preparedness Day outrage and all violence in all strikes in San Francisco.

The pamphlet was roundly applauded by members of the business community and universally damned by the unions. In its January 12, 1917 edition the *Labor Clarion* focused on the pamphlet and accused the Chamber of Commerce of distorting the facts:

The Chamber of Commerce of San Francisco has issued a printed statement covering the activities of its misnamed law and order committee which slanders the city, its public officials and its people. For down-right dishonesty and misrepresentation the publication is without parallel in the history of this city, and this city surely has had some experiences with vultures that prey upon humanity.[2]

In a succinct history of the Law and Order Committee, the *Labor Clarion* stated:

Pierced to the quick by the consciousness that the San Francisco wage workers were making real headway in their struggle for social justice, a band of pillagers who had used every weapon in the arsenal of greed to retard that progress met in the Merchants' Exchange Building last July and almost resolved to take over the government of the city from the properly constituted authorities and use its power to crush the organized toilers into the chains of subjection.[3]

Mayor Rolph was given the credit for having "punctured the bubble of the greedmongers."[4]

The report in the pamphlet of the death of a union striker was bitterly denounced by the unions. The pamphlet dismissed the murder of the striker as an act of self-defense. Union sources, principally the *Labor Clarion*, were quick to point out that the attack had been murder and that those responsible were even then on trial for the crime. Furthermore, the "historian" for the Committee had distorted the facts to give a false impression of the events in San Francisco in the last half of 1916. To the unions, the pamphlet proved that the Committee desired to "prostitute the functions of our municipal government to satisfy the soulless greed of its profit-crazed directors."[5]

One section of the pamphlet dealt with the work of the Law and Order Committee in Sacramento. During 1916 the Committee had tried to carry the open shop campaign to the state level as yet another dimension of the attack on the unions. If the fight for the open shop could receive throughout California the same kind of popular support it had received in San Francisco, the Committee would be on the road to a new career in politics. Its legitimacy, suspect by many in San Francisco, would be enhanced by a state-wide appeal and the possibilities above the state level were staggering.

The total muscle exerted by the Committee in Sacramento, however, was moderate. Though the Committee might have been successful with the winds of in-house politics in San Francisco, the halls of the State Legislature were somewhat different. The sum of its efforts resulted in negligible gains.

Of the four bills proposed by the Committee only one made it to the floor of the assembly. One was an antiboycott bill which would have outlawed the use of the "secondary boycott only." This would have been an effective weapon against the structural steel unions had it been passed.[6]

A second bill pushed by the Committee was an "Apprentice Bill" which would have made it a "misdemeanor" for anyone to "interfere with or prevent anyone from learning a skilled or useful trade." This act was aimed at stopping the unions from restricting entrance into certain professions. By limiting the number of apprentice workers the unions could, in effect, control the marketplace in that particular trade.[7]

The third bill which interested the Committee was known as the "Anti-Criminal Syndicalism" bill.[8] This act would have made it a felony to "teach or advocate crime, sabotage, violence or other unlawful methods of terrorism to bring about industrial or political reform." Although the provisions of this bill did not persuade the legislature to vote for its passage, in other forms this bill was to see a rather mephistophelian existence during the darker moments of the Great Red Scare barely two years over the horizon. Perhaps at that time the legislature might have looked back with nostalgia to the vain attempts of the Law and Order Committee.

The best luck the Committee had was with the proposed Public Utilities Mediation Act. This act was designed to suspend for up to 60 days any strike or lockout in regard to a public utility which served the public with "heat, light, water, power and means of transportation and communication."[9] This act, like the Anti-Criminal Syndicalism Bill, was premature. Two years later Calvin Coolidge would give life to the concept that there is "no right to strike against the public safety by anybody, anywhere, anytime." Much to the Committee's displeasure the act failed in the State Assembly by a vote of 52 to 16.[10]

In the final analysis the work of the Committee in Sacramento was an abysmal failure. But worse than a failure, it was embarrassing. From its defeats it was obvious to the Committee that it would never survive a state-wide campaign for the open shop. The primary impulse in San Francisco had been the Preparedness Day bombing. But this was merely a local issue and Chambers of Commerce in Los Angeles, Fresno, Sacramento and other California cities knew little and cared less about the bombing. To the labor unions it may have been a sacred cause to support Mooney and Billings, but to management organizations outside of the Bay area, their interest in the Mooney–Billings affair ended when it no longer made their local papers. Without any focus on the state level, the Committee's antilabor stand was just another of the many already in existence.

Secondly, though labor in California was not known to be a particularly powerful institution, the American Federation of Labor was able to push an anti-injunction bill through the legislature *while* the Committee was active in Sacramento.[11] This was a further embarrassment because, firstly, it had been introduced while the Committee had been pressing for antiunion measures and secondly, the bill had passed both Assembly and Senate whereas the Committee could not boast of even one bill through one house, let alone two. (The Committee did, however, help convince Governor Stephens to veto the bill when it reached his desk. There is substantial doubt, however, as to how influential the Committee actually was with the Governor.)

Back in San Francisco the Law and Order Committee had begun a long road to obscurity. With its failure in Sacramento the cry for the open shop had become weakened. In San Francisco the full power of the city administration had lined up with the unions against the Committee. By the end of January, and the collapse of the Structural Steel strike, the Law and Order Committee was without justification for existence. Rather than becoming a viable organization the Committee had been a stop-gap measure. The city-wide open shop was dead. The direct power of the Committee was quickly fading and the Chamber began to recede back to its prior policy of nonintervention in labor–management matters. There were a few battles yet to be fought but the muscle of the Law and Order Committee's campaign had been debilitated in Sacramento.

It was not until August of 1917 that the Law and Order Committee again took an active role against the unions. On August 22, 1917, the United Railroads workers went on strike. At a strategic moment some drivers suddenly stopped their streetcars and abandoned them. This created a monumental tie-up. The strike spread rapidly throughout the downtown area until most of the streetcars had been stopped. (San Francisco's transportation system ran with two owners: the United Railroads and the City of San Francisco. When the tie-up with the United Railroads occurred, the city cars were stopped as well. At one time Rolph had tried to buy the United Railroads lines in San Francisco so that the city would have a uniform system of transportation but this plan had been defeated by the San Francisco Board of Supervisors.)[12]

As the strike progressed, violence reminiscent of the previous year became everyday occurrences; the stoning of strikebreakers, destruction of property, sabotage and confrontations between strikers and strikebreakers once again brought violence to the streets of San Francisco. Within the first month there were more than 300 separate incidents of violence. One man had been killed. When the newspapers listed the acts of violence to date on September 8 it took more than seven columns of the paper to have them all included.[13]

For the Law and Order Committee the strike was the breath of life. Coming out strongly for more "law and order" along the United Railroads lines the Committee was quick to lay the blame for the death at the Mayor's doorstep regardless of the fact that the violence, in this case, had been because of the armed guards hired by the Committee. In an open letter advertisement in several of the city newspapers the Committee told Rolph

> your failure to perform your sworn duty has resulted in acts of violence including murder. The city knows that your failure is inexcusable and the record is indefensible.[14]

The *Argonaut*, once again supporting the Committee and the open shop, reproduced an editorial from the Sacramento *Bee* which claimed that Mayor Rolph "prostrates" himself and voluntarily "pampers thugism in fear of the union vote." "This," the *Argonaut* asserted, "is the bald truth."[15] More specifically, according to the *Argonaut*, there were four issues behind the Mayor's reluctance to enter the strike:

> (1) the United Railroads had "sustained" the use of the open shop and the unions wanted to "down it,"
> (2) the Mayor was playing politics for the labor vote in the next election,
> (3) the newspapers were "crawling on their bellies before the labor element" and

(4) there would be an attempt to force city ownership and operations of all the United Railroad lines that lay within the city limits.[16]

Basically there was more than a splinter of truth in the *Argonaut*'s contention. It can be assumed that the unions were interested in terminating the United Railroads open shop. There had been and would be in the future efforts to buy out the United Railroads. The city newspapers, in this strike, appeared to favor the unions whereas in the past their support had been lukewarm. In fact there was a great amount of sympathy for the strikers but as in the previous year, it was the violence that appalled the citizens of San Francisco and made any settlement better than no settlement at all. But the contention that Mayor Rolph was playing politics with the unions was a gross misrepresentation of the facts.

Within 48 hours Mayor Rolph published his reply in the city newspapers. In a direct attack on the Committee, Rolph contended that the hiring of the armed guards to protect the strikebreakers had been the initial cause of the violence. In direct reference to the Committee and Koster, Rolph stated:

> It is unfortunate that so many persons of your type ... are so incurably stupid and ignorant about business and industry, the very matters in which you are most concerned and in respect to which you deem yourself most enlightened.[17]

In direct reference to the murder, Rolph commented that the Committee was undoubtedly disappointed

> because the police have not turned machine guns on crowds in our streets and killed a few dozen strikers, including the usual number of bystanders.[18]

Although the Committee declined to respond to the Mayor's insinuation, the *Argonaut* was not reluctant to comment. Stating that it "would be the last to counsel resort to extra-legal and violent methods of dealing with official dereliction," it stated

> we can but recall that there was a day in San Francisco when men whose crimes against law and humanity were no less gross than those of Mayor Rolph were strung up by their dastard necks by

the hands of outraged decency amid the plaudits of the better elements of the community.[19]

The best way to end the violence the *Argonaut* asserted, would be to have "a single policeman stationed on each car" with orders to "shoot down whoever may assail" the car or the men operating it.[20]

Odd it was that the pendulum had swung so far back from the way it had come. Twelve months previously William McDevitt had made similar statements to a crowd at the Anti-Preparedness Day Rally and faced a trial because of his statements. No such fate was in store for the *Argonaut*. But in its declining age the Committee and its spokesman were resorting to the very tactics they condemned in others. The sign of a deteriorating campaign is the resort to calumny.

Again, as in the past, the Committee attempted to corral public support behind its position. In a badly botched attempt to have the president of the United Railroads, Patrick Calhoun, made an honorary member of the Chamber of Commerce, the Committee placed itself in a ridiculous position. Calhoun could have joined the Chamber merely by paying a membership fee. But the Committee, intent on using its prestige and Calhoun's name for publicity, pressed for "honorary" membership. This was particularly touchy since San Francisco was in the midst of the United Railroads strike and Calhoun carried with him not only the stigma of Big Business but corruption as well since he was then under indictment and was remembered by most from the Graft trials (see pages 11–12). A unanimous vote of the Board of Directors of the Chamber of Commerce was needed. Mayor Rolph, a member of that Board, would not vote in favor of the petition and it failed. Whether the Committee hoped to make a point of Rolph's refusal to vote or it assumed that he would approve Calhoun is not known. The union publications, however, greeted the absurd attempt with glee.[21]

The Committee also tried to gain the support of the community at large. In a special meeting between business leaders of San Francisco and the Chamber of Commerce on September 27, the Committee attempted to elicit support. One hundred and two delegates were present representing the Steamboat Owners' Association, Motor Car Dealers' Association, San Francisco Restaurant Association, San Francisco Real Estate Board, Wholesale Grocers' Association, San Francisco Advertising Club, Retail Lumber Dealers' Association, Home Industry League of California, Board of Trade of San Francisco, Rotary Club, Franklin Printing Trades Association, San

Francisco Commercial Club, San Francisco Chamber of Commerce, Building Industry Association, Retail Dry Goods Association of San Francisco, San Francisco Automobile Trade Association, General Contractors Association and the Building Materials Dealers' Association (see Appendix III). The Committee had prepared a petition that it hoped would be voted unanimously by the meeting. It appears that the Committee had learned from its disastrous meeting with the clergy the previous year. If the petitions were to be acceptable to any group of individuals it would have to be open enough to be acceptable to all. Thus the gathered businessmen voted to support the Law and Order Committee

> solely in the matter of restricting acts of violence through cooperation with the constituted authorities, in bringing about the preservation of law and order.[22]

This lukewarm statement was nothing less than a vote of confidence for the police and courts of San Francisco, but it was undoubtedly the strongest statement the Committee could have hoped to have passed this body.

The Committee should have received two messages from this gathering. Firstly, it was a gathering of mid-sized businesses. These were the businesses who stood to gain the most by the open shop. They were not the huge corporations like United Railroads, Standard Oil, Santa Fe and Southern Pacific or Wells Fargo Nevada National Bank. These were the mid-level businesses whose assets and branch offices were all in the San Francisco area. They represented the lifeblood of the Committee's support, as they stood to gain the most by an open shop. Whereas 12 months earlier they had wholeheartedly supported the Law and Order campaign, in September of 1917, however, the Committee was an effete embarrassment. Secondly, whether by design or accident, the Chamber of Commerce was listed as a participant—not a compeer of the Law and Order Committee. Perhaps the Chamber too was finding the Law and Order Committee a burden rather than a blessing.

In the midst of the violence of the United Railroads strike, a new voice spoke out on behalf of labor: Matthew I. Sullivan, chief justice of the Supreme Court of California. Sullivan, speaking at a public rally for the Mission Promotion Association, gave a lengthy and critical analysis of the Law and Order Committee and its campaign. Dubbing Koster and the Committee as "Kaiser Koster and his associates" Sullivan accused them of "circulating wildly untruthful reports of 'riots' and 'outrages' in the street car strike." Included in Sullivan's tirade was S. Fred Hogue, an investigative reporter for the *Los Angeles Times* who was working "hand in glove with Kaiser Koster and his associates" in a course bent on "assassination of the character and reputation" of Mayor Rolph. It was Sullivan's contention that Hogue was responsible for "lying accounts of the situation in San Francisco and vilifying in the most scurrilous manner Mayor Rolph and his administration." Hogue's alleged intent was because

> The papers of San Francisco did not exaggerate sufficiently the acts of violence committed during the present strike; they did not furnish enough "blood and thunder" to satisfy the demands of the Law and Order Committee, so that Committee called to its assistance the Los Angeles Times, the arch enemy of labor and the most vicious enemy of our city—a sheet that for years past has slandered San Francisco for the miserably selfish purpose of helping Los Angeles.

Sullivan then gave an example of a falsehood perpetuated by Hogue. The *Los Angeles Times* printed a story concerning the attack on a strikebreaker as follows:

> Nickolas Schaack is the father of a family living at No. 125 Precita Avenue. He is 52 years of age and has been an employee of the United Railroads for thirteen years. Schaack is in the St. Francis Hospital, probably blinded for life. When he was attacked by the Jack Murphy coyote gang last Wednesday night they tore one of his eyes from his head and threw it on the street; the other was gouged out of its socket and lay on his cheek, but surgical specialists have replaced it and he can now distinguish daylight from darkness. His nose is broken, his jaw is fractured and two ribs are broken. That he still lives and is able to relate his experience is a marvel.

Sullivan claimed that the story was false because Schaack merely had both eyes "blackened." Sullivan further asserted that both of Schaack's eyes were in their sockets when he went to the hospital. This type of representation, Sullivan charged, is a "revolting falsehood" typical of the "lies that have been deliberately circulated throughout the State of California by the *Los Angeles Times*."

In defense of the *Los Angeles Times*, however, it must be added that nowhere in Sullivan's speech is there a further reference to Nickolas or Victor—as Sullivan contends his name was—Schaack. According to Sullivan's speech Schaack was an employee of the United Railroads. But nowhere does Sullivan concede that the incident related in the *Los Angeles Times* was strike-related.

As far as the city of San Francisco was concerned, Sullivan asserted that the Law and Order Committee was guilty of pigeonholing industrial surveys (see next chapter), and of hampering the attempts of civil authorities to maintain law and order. In actual fact, he claimed, the civic concerns of the Chamber of Commerce were

> a mere camouflage used to conceal a masked battery whose guns are directed against organized labor and incidently against Mayor Rolph and his administration.

Sullivan denounced the Chamber of Commerce for allowing such a committee to exist and then proceeded to disclose the names of the top 23 contributors (see Appendix IV).* Sullivan concluded with a threat

> If the Law and Order Committee wishes to prosecute to a finish the war which it has begun, let it be war, but war without violence: and I assure you that victory will come to the side that has the greatest number—not the greatest number of dollars, but the greatest number of decent, law-abiding citizens, the vast majority of whom are with, and will remain with, Mr. Rolph in this fight.

The speech was so well received that two San Francisco newspapers, the San Francisco *Daily News* and San Francisco *Bulletin*, published it in its entirety. The *Daily News* strategically placed the following filler at the end of Sullivan's speech:

> Notwithstanding the indictments against him and notwithstanding the universally known fact that Patrick Calhoun was the arch corruptionist among those who had debauched public

It is a point to ponder that although Sullivan claimed to have named 23 contributors he only named 22. Many have wondered if Sullivan was incorrect in his statement or he "neglected" to name a firm at the last moment.

officials during the Schmitz regime, fourteen members of the
board of directors of the Chamber of Commerce — all men of high
standing and respectability — voted to elect Patrick Calhoun
honorary member. Mr. Rolph stood out alone against his conferes
[sic] on the board and voted "No." Calhoun could not receive the
unanimous vote and he was therefore prevented from becoming
an honorary member of that august body which has given birth to
the Law and Order Committee.[23]

Despite the rhetoric and an expenditure of more than $40,000, the striking unions only succeeded in slowing down the United Railroads. Schedules had been erratic for several days after the strike was called but within a short period of time schedules returned to normal. With the help of the Law and Order Committee, nonunion labor was supplied and armed guards protected them.[24] But the key factor in the collapse of the United Railroads strike was that the citizens of San Francisco were apathetic toward the unions and this, in the final analysis, was the outstanding factor in the termination of the strike.

As a corpse the Committee was a lively one. But its last confrontation was, ironically, related to the case which gave it life: the Mooney–Billings affair. By the end of 1917 the Law and Order Committee had no vitality left and rather than fighting for its survival, the Committee had been reduced to fighting for credibility in the campaign it had already lost. Odd it was that this affair had at first given the Law and Order Committee a platform to carry on the campaign for the open shop and in the final days of its existence it was the Mooney–Billings affair that finished it.

The trial of Mooney and Billings had been marred from the beginning. Intimidation of witnesses, illegal searches and seizures, blackmail and the manufacturing of evidence were but a few of the outrages perpetrated at the trials of the two labor organizers. Sixty years after the affair there is little doubt that the two were innocent and it remains to be proven whether anyone other than the notorious district attorney for the City and County of San Francisco, Charles M. Fickert, was actively involved in the frame-up. But there have been insinuations that the Law and Order Committee, which worked very closely with District Attorney Fickert throughout the investigation of the bombing and the trials which followed, worked hand-in-glove in the frame-up. And even if this were not true, the Committee was so inextricably tied with the District Attorney and the

Mooney–Billings affair that it must be assumed that some of the taint of a frame-up rubbed off on its reputation.

Though Mooney and Billings had been sentenced there was a general uproar in labor and radical circles over the fact that the two had been framed. If this was true the Law and Order Committee with their close association with the prosecution stood to be held culpable before the law.

The fate of the case hinged on the testimony of Frank Oxman, the key witness in the trials. It was Oxman's testimony that actually placed Mooney at the scene of the crime. Later a photograph showed Mooney more than a mile from the scene of the crime but Oxman's testimony seemed to carry more weight in court. The testimony held until April of 1917.

Oxman, in an effort to maintain his own credibility, had written to a friend, F.E. Rigall, and asked him to come to San Francisco. In the letter Oxman had written:

> I [Oxman] have a chance for you to come to San Francisco as an expert witness. You will only have to say that you seen me July 22d. You will only have to answer three or four questions. I will post you on what to say and that will be easy done.

When Fickert was asked to comment on Oxman's letter, Fickert issued a statement condemning Mooney and Billings. But the evidence was strong enough to select a grand jury to determine if Oxman should stand trial for perjury. When Oxman was tried, three-quarters of the grand jury were members of the San Francisco Chamber of Commerce. Oxman's lawyer, Samuel M. Shortridge, was the personal attorney for John D. Spreckles, foreman of the grand jury. By a vote of 14 to 3 the grand jury found "no cause for criticism of the District Attorney's office."[25] There have been many who questioned this proceeding.

By November of 1917 a coalition of Mooney–Billings supporters and San Francisco labor groups felt they had enough support to bring forth a petition for the recall of District Attorney Fickert. For the Law and Order Committee the situation turned from desperate to critical. If the petitioners succeeded in placing the recall on the ballot the very heart of the Committee's credibility would be in jeopardy. But the situation was now not a matter of merely defending credibility but perhaps even a matter of staying out of jail. In desperation, it would seem, the Committee fought the recall.

The raising of the signatures on the petitions had been a slow and arduous process marked with violence and chicanery virtually every step of the way. Fickert, with the help of the Law and Order Committee, fought the recall as best he could. Petition bearers were beaten and their petitions destroyed. Some solicitors were accused by Fickert of having forged names on their petitions; these solicitors were indicted. Fickert even took the petitions to court as being invalid. The court was unimpressed and refused to rule in his favor.[26]

In this last fight the Committee once again used its tremendous power as a civic organization to defend Fickert. In personal letters from Koster and the Committee to many of the most influential members of the San Francisco community, Koster spoke of the attempt by Anarchist powers to subvert the American process by trying to recall Fickert. In full page newspaper advertisements the Law and Order Committee defended Fickert in spite of his questionable activities. (Even the *Argonaut* admitted that Fickert was a man of "rather dull sensibilities and a slow mentality."[27]) The ads were meant to tie Fickert as close to anti-Anarchism and antiradicalism as possible:

> The Chamber of Commerce without taking partisan stand considers it its duty to define the real issues to its members. Whatever the character or ability of the District Attorney, if this attack upon his office succeeds, FULL NOTICE WILL BE GIVEN TO THE ENTIRE COUNTRY THAT THIS CITY IS OPPOSED TO THE PROSECUTION OF ANARCHISTS, and the hands of every IWW and lawless element in the United States will be strengthened in this time of national crisis, and the forces of lawlessness will be accordingly stimulated, San Francisco will be understood as a community in which red-handed anarchism goes unrebuked.[28]

Though the recall was fated to be very, very close, two factors helped tip the balance. Just before the balloting a telegram addressed to Fickert from former President Theodore Roosevelt was printed in the San Francisco *Chronicle*. This unexpected—and crucial—endorsement read in part:

> I am informed that an effort is being made to recall you because you have successfully prosecuted the anarchists who during the Preparedness Day parade killed ten persons and injured sixty others.

If such be the fact, I not only feel that the issue between you and your opponents is that between patriotism and anarchy, but I also feel that all who directly or indirectly assail you for any reason should be promptly deprived of their citizenship.[29]

Whether Roosevelt was aware of the actual situation in San Francisco is not known. But even if he had recanted the image of the telegram had made its impression.

Yet another irony entered into the fate of the Law and Order Committee. On the night before the recall a bomb went off in the home of Governor Stephens. Though this was in no way, as far as anyone knows, related to any San Francisco person, strike or recall, it undoubtedly served to change many minds over the recall. Tremors of hindsight undoubtedly shook many voters for the next day the polls were flooded with 30,000 unexpected voters. The recall was beaten easily.

The Committee was still influential. On July 16, 1918, the Committee forced Fremont Older to resign from the San Francisco *Bulletin*. Older had been continually advised by the owners of the *Bulletin* that his consistent focus on the Mooney–Billings affair was inadvisable but Older continued to scoop the other San Francisco papers on most of the developments of the Mooney case. On July 16, 1918, Older submitted his resignation rather than cease following the ever widening trail of the Mooney–Billings frame-up.[30] Although the *Argonaut* rejoiced that the "evil genius" of the *Bulletin* had left, William Randolph Hearst was quick to hire Older. In a personal telegram to Older, Hearst offered Older the editorship of the San Francisco *Call and Post* and to "bring the Mooney case with you."[31]

With the defeat of the recall the Committee's purpose was ended. Its questionable activities beginning to be questioned, many people were convinced that the Committee would best be left behind in the history of San Francisco rather than the legal annals of the State. There was a general feeling that the Committee had become diseased with the very virus it had sought to exterminate. Koster, who had been the driving genius behind the Committee, conveniently began neglecting the Committee for an extended speaking tour across the United States and subsequently a series of Federal posts. In August of 1919, during his absence, the *coup de grace* was delivered — the Chamber of Commerce formally dissolved the Law and Order Committee of the San Francisco Chamber of Commerce.[32]

Civic Reaction
to the Committee

Civic reaction to the Law and Order Committee was divided. It was not as though the city had split along some hypothetical, ideological line but it would be more accurate to say that the support of the Committee was capricious. The unions, of course, were unalterably, immutably, uncompromisingly opposed to the Law and Order Committee, its program, its campaign, its membership and its backers. The Law and Order Committee was the devil incarnate; it was the apogee of avarice; it was the foe in a modern Armageddon with which no quarter would be expected or given.

But the sentiment of the public, those persons who were not directly associated with the unions or the Chamber of Commerce, was more inclined to be pro-Committee. Unlike the unions, there was a general feeling in the closing days of 1916 that the Committee was a respectable organization dedicated to "law and order." The hysteria of the Preparedness Day bombing and the Mooney-Billings affair gave the Committee a longevity which it neither expected nor appreciated and with each strike the Committee seemed to kick away some segment of the public support it strived so desperately to consolidate. From strike to strike and month to month the Committee's influence in San Francisco eroded. Though many viewed the Committee as an atavistic child of the committees of vigilance of the previous century, most San Franciscans saw the Committee as the natural outcropping of the demand for "law and order" by a group of citizens. If there was a cabal behind the Committee, the man in the street did not see it. And, after all, who was to express the citizens' point of view of the labor-management confrontation if the Mayor and the city administration refused to take a firm stand. The most important factor concerning the Committee's credibility with the general public was that there were very few attempts by the general public to stop the Law and Order Committee, its program or its campaign. With the exception of a petition and an outraged statement it appears that the citizens of San Francisco let the Committee run its course. By the doctrine of *tacit consent* it may be assumed that the citizens of San Francisco backed the Committee.

Civil organizations were also divided. An example might be the San Francisco Board of Supervisors, the most powerful body in San Francisco when it wished to exercise its power. Under the assumption that anonymity was the greatest asset and best defense from controversy, the Board preferred to remain on the sidelines. In most of the labor disputes in 1916 the Board was a tacit ally of the Committee. This, however, is not to say it was pro-Committee. Although it never publicly stated its position or preference, in many instances the Board sided with the Chamber of Commerce. But, in all fairness, it must be added that because some of the members of the Board were businessmen it would be expected that they would view the matters from a businessman's point of view rather than a worker's perspective.

An example of the power of the Board might be seen in the struggle to control the United Railroads lines in San Francisco. One of Mayor Rolph's pet projects was to buy out the United Railroads in San Francisco—a desire eventually consummated in 1917—and make them part of a municipal concern. As United Railroads was a combination of different lines, Rolph recognized the need to create a single, city-run conglomerate for transportation. The Board of Supervisors, however, was opposed to such a proposition and when Rolph attempted to buy out the United Railroads he was temporarily blocked by the Board. Had this sale transpired earlier there might not have been a United Railroads strike in 1917.[1]

The Board of Supervisors was also responsible for the initiation of the antipicketing ordinance. When this passed in November of 1916, it brought a rapid end to the Culinary strike then in progress and created a major stumbling block for any future strikes within the city limits. The Board quietly avoided any confrontation with the unions by omitting the discussion of the ordinances in its preelection voter guides. When the unions finally did begin to harass the Board to take a stand, it effectively ducked the issue in what was said to be the best interest of "the mayor's political machine for the upcoming election."[2]

Mayor Rolph, unlike other civil officials, was both free and willing to throw himself into the fray. Being a businessman himself he was sensitive to the concerns of the business community. At the same time he was an astute political observer and he was keenly aware that the power of the labor unions was enough to tip the balance in any election, a lesson Charles Evans Hughes would rue. In the conflicts Rolph tried to retain a neutral stand in spite of his personal feelings. Rather than disliking the Committee, it could be said that Rolph found its position distasteful and an encroachment on his domain. In July of 1916 Rolph addressed biting words to Koster over the budding campaign of the Law and Order Committee:

> Permit me to say, in the first place, that neither you nor the Law and Order Committee of the Chamber of Commerce has earned by any conspicious devotion to law and order, the right to lecture me or the Police Department. On the contrary, the attitude and the activities of you and your particular group have done much, in my opinion, to engender industrial unrest and class hatred culminating on a few occasions in turbulence and violence, which lately distressed this community.[3]

Later Rolph uttered another disparagement of the Committee:

> I am sure that not even a considerable minority of our people is in sympathy with any campaign to destroy organized labor—a movement which precipitates a wasteful and distressful struggle, which brings no good to anyone and divides the community for years.[4]

But within the city administration Rolph had a unique position. If he, as mayor of San Francisco, decided to throw his weight into any business–labor confrontation, he carried with him the entire force of the city's administration. Rolph, like Koster, was the head of an organization that followed where he led. Any other civil servant further down the bureaucratic stepladder could conceivably have found his job in jeopardy by entering a controversial dispute—even as an individual.

Another sector of the community which was anything but unanimous in its point of view concerning the Law and Order Committee was the San Francisco press. In every single case the *Argonaut*, undaunted by facts or insinuations, supported the Committee. Its coverage of the Committee was complete and it rarely failed to color the Committee in the hue of a noble crusader in battle with the fire-breathing dragon. Often the *Argonaut* represented the emotional "soul" of the Committee which yearned for a platform.

Other newspapers were as capricious as the public. The San Francisco *Chronicle* and the San Francisco *Examiner* were usually supportive of the Committee though this support was quite often lukewarm. In the United Railroads Strike, for instance, the *Chronicle* and the *Examiner* surprised their pundits by supporting the strikers. The San Francisco *Call and Post*, San Francisco *Bulletin*, *Coast Seaman's Journal* and the *Labor Clarion* were consistent critics of the Committee.

Then there was *The Blast*. With the possible exception of the *Argonaut* there was no other newspaper in the city of San Francisco that the unions feared more than *The Blast*. Nothing can be more dangerous than a dimwitted friend. Every prolabor article in *The Blast* was another nail in the union's coffin. As the Mooney–Billings trials became a clearcut case of labor vs. business, the labor press began to carefully choose its allies. In an attempt to consolidate all of the "legitimate," i.e., nonradical, sentiment, the *Labor Clarion* spoke for the labor community and urged the radicals to join the more established labor organizations:

> If the radicals really have the interest of the Labor movement at heart, they will shun these outsiders whose innocent dupes they have been, and will join in hands with the tried and true trade unionists in an effort to build up and improve the Labor Council and its affiliated unions.[5]

The radical press, however, felt otherwise. Such advice was tantamount to stating that anyone who was a radical was misguided. *The Blast*, the most widely read radical journal in San Francisco, supported the unions unfailingly and most often to an embarrassing extent. *The Blast*, however, was for immediate confrontation and its name seemed to indicate the method. This merely added fuel to the Law and Order Committee's assertion that "law and order" was tragically absent in San Francisco. It was the policy of *The Blast* to carry the case of labor, Tom Mooney and Warren Billings to the court of public opinion. To Berkman,

> The San Francisco cases are not local successes or defeats. They will quickly show [their] effects on the labor struggle in the whole country.

But Berkman was a dreamer. When he went to New York in late 1916 he was "surprised to find that the situation on the coast [San Francisco] was practically unknown even to the radical element."[7]

Berkman learned in New York what Koster had learned in Sacramento: the Mooney–Billings hysteria was a matter of concern only in San Francisco. Although Mooney and Billings were saved from the gas chamber, it was through a non-San Francisco rally—a protest in Moscow. But this only showed that the radicals, unlike the Law and Order Committee, were organized beyond the city limits of San Francisco and not that they were particularly powerful anywhere, least of all in San Francisco.

Writing in New York, for instance, Robert Minor wrote of the Mooney–Billings affair for Emma Goldman's *Mother Earth*:

> The newspapers [in San Francisco] are always crooked, but in this particular case it would amaze even a "cynical" red to see the audacity with which they lied. It was so unanimous that the editors took courage in their numbers and frankly told us, face to face, that they couldn't print anything that didn't have the approval of the Committee on Law and Order of the Chamber of Commerce. One newspaperman of high position on a conservative paper came to me, secretly, to say "I am writing every day under orders in a way deliberately calculated to hang those men; and they are not guilty.[8]

Eugue V. Debs, writing for the *International Socialist Review* in Chicago, said of the Committee:

> The plundering plutocrats' thirst to lap Tom Mooney's honest blood must be thwarted. These hyenas shall not break his neck and gloat over his dead body. Their infamous court and its filthy hirelings have brought them bound and gagged to the gallows but they shall not chortle over his ghastly murder.[9]

But the radicals' support of labor in San Francisco was in rhetoric only. Though their press' integrity and accuracy is questionable, it is important to note that the radical press carried news that other papers could not, or would not, print. These newspapers had what other presses dream of, a truly national subscription. From the listing of donations for the Mooney–Billings affair printed on the back of *The Blast* it is astonishing to note that though the coverage was notably biased the readership was dedicated.

There were others who opposed the Law and Order Committee. Surprisingly there was opposition to the Committee in some of the higher echelons of the city. Resignations from the Committee and the Chamber, though not explicitly for opposition to the open shop fight, were numerous in 1916 and 1917. R.I. Bentley, one of the Chamber's best industrial experts, resigned in September of 1916. No reason was given for his resignation. In November of the same year C.F. Michaels, one of the five executive members of the Law and Order Committee, resigned because of "illness." The Reverend C.S.S. Dutton had resigned his membership on the Committee of One Hundred soon after he had learned of his appointment.[10]

But the greatest disapproval came from within the Chamber of Commerce itself. In August of 1916, a formal statement protesting the Law and Order Committee had been introduced in the Chamber, with 279 members signing it.[11] As the Law and Order campaign began to gain momentum, resignations from the Chamber began to climb. In 1915 there had been 207 resignations and cancellations. In 1916 there had been 186. But in 1917 the figure jumped to an astonishing 545 resignations and cancellations. This was an enormous increase over the previous year. (This figure is *low* because all resignations and cancellations for October, November and December were entered in the San Francisco Chamber of Commerce Minutes as "listed as accepted and approved."[12] Unlike previous months, no figures were given after September, 1917—perhaps even to this day.) In the six months from January to July of 1917 there was an increase in the rate of resignations and cancellations over four and half times that of the previous six months (see Appendix V).

The Law and Order Committee also created problems for itself with the various industrial surveys it financed. At least two surveys were made of the San Francisco economic situation but neither of them was released. Dr. B.M. Rastall, the "foremost business expert in the United States, and a man of national reputation," had been commissioned for $10,000 to conduct a survey of the industrial conditions of San Francisco. Rastall finished his survey and reported that, among other items of interest to both labor and management, San Francisco paid a higher wage than many other parts of the country but this higher wage "does not seem to materially increase manufacturing costs."[13] Much to the disappointment of the Committee, the unions applauded the survey as justification that the strikes for an increase in pay would not harm the industrial capacity of San Francisco. The report, however, was never released. The San Francisco *Bulletin* quoted extensively from the survey but the report was not made public.

The suppression of a second survey was more deliberate. Until 1973, the Miner Chipman Industrial Survey was believed to have been lost. Then, entirely by accident, it was discovered in the archives of the Library of Industrial Relations at the John F. Kennedy School of Government, Harvard University.[14]

Miner Chipman had been hired by the Law and Order Committee in May of 1917 to conduct an impartial survey of the "industrial conditions" of San Francisco. His qualifications for such a task are difficult to ascertain because prior to the San Francisco survey the only documented work he had completed was the presentation of a paper entitled "Efficiency, Scientific Management and Organized Labor" to the National Efficiency Society in 1916. Possibly this presentation was the recommendation that secured him the Committee's appointment. The survey began in May, 1917, but by October an impasse had been reached between Chipman and the Committee resulting in Chipman's being informed that the Committee "deemed" it a wise course of action to "discontinue the study." The survey was submitted December 5, 1917, seven months short of its originally intended scope, and subsequently pigeonholed. It reappeared in June of 1947 when it was donated to the Library of Industrial Relations.

The Chipman survey was a cataloging of complaints made by the unions about the employers and vice versa which concluded with the author's remarks on the industrial condition of San Francisco. The survey was divided into four sections: the first detailed the "case against" the employers, the labor unions and the public. The second section dealt with the "answers" of the employers, labor unions and the public. The third section dealt with the "responsibility" of the previously named three parties and the final section dealt with the "remedy" for the industrial situation as it existed.

The report, however, is an historian's nightmare. The grammar of the manuscript is faulty. The organization is chaotic. Allusions are cryptic and sometimes difficult to decipher and the report is so opinionated that it is difficult to interpret the facts from the vituperations. But, with these shortcomings aside, the survey did bring to light many of the major complaints and paranoias which were widespread in San Francisco in 1917.

The central theme of the survey was the denunciation of extremism in San Francisco: both union and employer oriented. In regard to the unions, Chipman condemned them for establishing a policy of "temporary expedience" as a foundation for "permanent success" in shop conditions and wage negotiations. Though he excused the individual union members from complete responsibility for the complex state of affairs, he chastised them for being the "dupe of fallacious doctrines of political economy." He further defined "political economy" as the state of affairs where a union leader could use his position as a stepladder to political office.[15]

This was not a new theme in San Francisco labor history. The plight of the union member in the hands of a politicized union leader was a clever device used to condemn unionization but condone the workmen. Hubert Howe Bancorft, the eminent California historian, in *Modern Fallacies* (1915), was quite caustic in his description of the politicized union leaders. Labelling them as "exploiters" of unions, he claimed that they urged their members to strike and boycott "honest businessmen."[16] From a radically different source, Alexander Berkman, writing in *Mother Earth*, was far less restrained than either Chipman or Bancroft when he attacked San Francisco as a city where unions were merely "stepping stones for the advancement of political charlatans and labor grafters."[17]

Chipman went into great detail concerning these union leaders and their imperfections. In discussing their numerous vices, he divided his subject into five categories with only one dealing with a "competent" union leader. (Even the "competent" union leader had a streak of Machiavellianism for although his "motives cannot be impeached" his methods were to be "seriously questioned.") The remaining four stereotypes characterized the union leader in various hues of corruption, politicization, incompetence and venality.[18]

In the survey's only specific, concrete example, Chipman attempted to illustrate the epitome of the incompetent labor leader by stating what he witnessed during the hearing of the Iron Trades Council before the United States Wage Control Board:

> When the Board convened, and the meeting was called to order, Chairman Macy called upon labor to present its case. IT HAD NONE. Not a scrap of paper, not a line, not a word, absolutely NOTHING—that was the Case of Labor.[19]

There is reason, however, to doubt this account. In November of the previous year, 1916, Rolph had called an arbitration session to be held between the striking iron workers and their employers (see pages 84–89). At that time William Michels, secretary of the Housesmiths and Architectural Iron Workers Local 38, wrote a competent attack on the stand of the employers. Point by point he showed that the stand of the employers seemed to be based on a single desire: the establishment of the open shop. It would seem unlikely that six months later the unions could have become so impotent with such excellent groundwork prepared.

The most debatable point of the entire survey, and possibly the reason that the survey was not made public, was a list of allegations against the Law and Order Committee. A careful analysis of the 23 allegations made against the employers revealed that 83 percent of the applicable complaints dealt exclusively with the Law and Order Committee and the open shop campaign.

Included in the complaints made by the unions were the usual charges of employers being "behind the times," the hiring of strikebreakers, the insistence on the open shop and the suspicions that employers spied on their workmen. These had been voiced by the unions since the turn of the century, but in 1916, the new and nefarious ingredient was the Law and Order Committee.

But Chipman's compilation is enigmatic for it implies that at the heart of the industrial tension was the Law and Order Committee, *not* the employers. The Committee obviously had the backing of the business community. Big Business was represented by the Committee as can be attested by the list of donors released by Sullivan. The mid-sized businesses supported the Committee as can be shown by a representative sample in the meeting of September 19, 1917. The smashing success of the membership drive would also tend to indicate that the smaller businesses were in favor of the Committee. The obvious conclusion to be drawn is that the business community did indeed support the Law and Order Committee. Though the business community supported the Committee, the unions apparently continued to distinguish between the two parties.

One of the only instances of public opposition from any large business came from the First National Bank in San Francisco. When the list of donors had been released by Sullivan, Rudolph Spreckles was outraged to find that the bank of which he was president had made a healthy donation. Spreckles demanded the return of the donation. The controversy continued to build and finally culminated with the resignation of one bank director and threats of more resignations if the donation was not returned.[20] When the rhetoric died, the donation remained with the Committee.

In his conclusion, Chipman summed up the charges that had been made against the unions and the employers. He ascertained that the strife in San Francisco was not due to the dubious actions of either participant, but to the neglect of both. Both labor and management viewed the confrontation as a life-and-death struggle whose outcome would only be acceptable if their view prevailed. At the center of the conflict was the complicating factor: differing personalities whose personal recalcitrance doomed any negotiations. Thus the chances for the settlement of the city-wide conflicts were dim. Chipman obviously viewed the situation as hopeless as he suggested for the remedy: "?".[21]

His suggestions for the employers were biting. Although the blame for the industrial unrest was shared by both management and labor, the bulk of the responsibility lay with the employers. It was pointed out that the weakness of the employers as a collective organization was the sole reason that the unions were so powerful. The attempts by the employers to form a viable organization were commendable, but had backfired as the employers supported cabals which aroused suspicion rather than confidence. Chipman cut the foundation out from under the Committee by making it clear that law and order was not the exclusive property of any group. Law and order was a "civic" responsibility. Chipman also made it clear that hysteria was the primary cause for the unrest that plagued San Francisco. For the public he had no recommendations. For the unions his recommendations were succinct:

(1) LAW AND ORDER.
(2) Democracy and self-government.
(3) The Industrial Prosperity of San Francisco.
(4) Competency of Leadership.
(5) Efficiency and high wages.

For the future, though he could suggest no remedy for the present, Chipman suggested that the Chamber transform the Law and Order Committee into a "clearing house" for information regarding industrial affairs.[22] In its present condition the Committee was a pernicious influence.

It cannot be denied that the Chipman survey was prounion. That it lacked professionalism is also undeniable. But whether these shortcomings begat his being relieved of the study or the other way around is a matter of conjecture. One might wonder if the prounion position was based on studies or personal chagrin.

The Law and Order Committee also drew criticism from social

organizations in San Francisco. The Civic League of Improvement Clubs and Associations, a public service organization, conducted an investigation of the Chamber in 1919. It was the league's conclusion that the Chamber of Commerce was being dominated by the Law and Order Committee, which was "selfish and opposed to the civic welfare of San Francisco."[23]

The San Francisco Center, the forerunner of the San Francisco League of Women Voters, an organization that had always been bold in taking a civic stand when the majority of members consented, was strangely silent. In April of 1917, a woman supporting a "Committee of Citizens," a group of private citizens who took a public stand against the Law and Order Committee, allowed her name to be used with the title "San Francisco Center" following it. Soon after the advertisement for the "Committee of Citizens" appeared in the San Francisco *Examiner*, the San Francisco Center sent letters to the Chamber of Commerce, the San Francisco Labor Council and the San Francisco *Examiner* disavowing any part in the advertisement. Furthermore, the San Francisco Center stated that it did not wish to be involved in this "controversy." This incident tends to suggest that the San Francisco Center, like the citizenship of San Francisco, was split.[24]

Even in the city administration there was ambivalence. The Police Department, a key organization in the open shop campaign, appeared split. While the mayor of San Francisco could be satisfied with lofty ideals, it was the patrolman on the street who was undoubtedly more favorable to the aims of the Committee. It was the police, not the mayor, who had to contend with the violence. It was the patrolman who had to inventory the dismembered corpses while the closest the mayor came to the outrages was a list of injuries. Any organization that would reduce the violence in the streets would be sure to find enthusiastic supporters in the Police Department.

But there were other sections of the Police Department who were not as enthusiastic. In an independent survey for the San Francisco Real Estate Board by a New York firm, the subject of arrests was covered for fiscal year 1915. Excluding cases of intoxication, 34,603 arrests were made. But 83 percent of them were discharged in police courts. In all felony cases only 30 percent resulted in conviction.[25] One conclusion could be that the patrolmen were arresting far more people than their own courts were willing to process.

The Police Department was split. While the patrolman was busy keeping the peace, the police judges were far more inclined to be lenient with lawbreakers, especially union lawbreakers. In San Francisco the union votes would go heavily in favor of a judge who had proved to be somewhat sympathetic toward strikers. The Law and Order Committee was well aware of this proclivity and installed a special attorney, E. Porter Ashe, to "look into the police courts."[26]

As far as the business community was concerned, the Law and Order Committee was their representative. As the chicanery began to become public knowledge, the Committee began to lose popularity but for the businessman the Committee was the focus which was so desperately needed by the business community that it was willing to back a committee of vigilance. Solidarity was the key to success. The unions were organized. The business community was not. But in spite of the fact that the business community was split, many businessmen and merchants felt that the Committee was the best that could be expected under the circumstances. It was not a perfect representative by any means but it was the only representative they had.

The Demise of the Committee

It was indisputable that the Law and Order Committee was a viable organization. For more than a year, from July of 1916 to August of 1917, the Law and Order Committee carried on the open shop campaign with virtual impunity. But why, at the height of its popularity, should it suddenly deteriorate? April of 1917 brought World War I and patriotism became the vogue. Would this not have given the Committee a boost? In November of 1917 the Russian Revolution showed the world that *it, the revolution*, could happen. Would this not have added to the Committee's credibility?

The primary reason for the failure of the Committee was the First World War. In mid-1916 the open shop battle was in full swing. But as the war boom brought more and more money into the coffers of San Francisco businessmen, the business community felt less pressed to fight the unions. Scab labor which had proven so significant in the lockouts of the previous years had proved itself to be too unskilled to take the place of union workers for any length of time. Even if the struck firm did continue to produce its product, the quality of the product suffered.

As the war progressed the financial losses of the businesses began to increase with each strike. A strike in 1917 could have resulted in losses many times greater than a strike of the same duration the previous year. Gradually the desire for the open shop was overridden by the desire for financial successes.

Between 1909 and 1919, San Francisco's trade increased by 274 percent while in the same period the national increase was only 107 percent. In 1916 alone, the second six months of the year showed a 40 percent increase over the previous six. In spite of the strikes, San Francisco was still involved in commercial traffic. Exports from San Francisco were 56 percent higher than in 1915. Bank clearings in 1916 had increased by nearly one billion dollars making San Francisco the leading banking center on the Pacific Coast. The nearest competitor was Los Angeles which had total bank clearings 50 percent less than that of San Francisco.[1]

Along with the increase in trade there was an increase in the demand for labor. The Bethlehem Iron Works expanded its work force twelve times between 1915 and 1919. Navy yards began appearing in San Francisco Bay when the Navy issued contracts for a fleet to be built in San Francisco. The Union Iron Works was given a contract for $7 million to build torpedo boats. A $10 million bond issue was passed by the state to increase the dock area in San Francisco to make room for the new activity.[2] With the money in Federal contracts came the demand for skilled labor and the materials to build.

The geographic isolation of San Francisco also forced the city to solve its own problems. Local unions and businessmen had to depend on themselves rather than on an outside mediator. When a Federal mediator was sent to San Francisco, the local unions often did not feel bound by national agreements but only by local negotiations. This attitude further isolated the San Francisco unions from their national organizations.[3] As a result the San Francisco unions increased their power until local businessmen felt uncomfortable in their shadow. Without an ally, the business community welcomed the birth of the Law and Order Committee.

But the isolation made labor hard to find. San Francisco had little nonunion labor immediately available to replace strikers. Men would often have to be hired from as far away as Chicago and New Orleans.[4] The transportation of these men was expensive and there was always the possibility that the imported scabs would join the unions. Once unionized this vast supply of manpower was a potent weapon in the hands of the unions.

In order to "organize" nonunion labor, the Law and Order Committee founded the American Stevedore Company to keep nonunion labor ready for immediate use. It was the Committee's strategy to keep this pool in San Francisco, hopeful of course, that it was cheaper to maintain scabs than to import them. But the Committee did not seem concerned that the strikebreakers produced a poor quality of products.

World War I also brought a change to the Chamber of Commerce. Koster was appointed to a Federal post and his position as president of the Chamber of Commerce fell to Atholl McBean who led the Chamber away from the dominating influence of the Committee.[5] Once back in its traditional role as a neutral observer in labor disputes, the Chamber limited its involvement to passing resolutions and exerting civic pressures.*

*It is interesting to note that Prohibition might have been a cause for the

The overall accomplishment of the Law and Order Committee can best be summed up by examining two passages from the San Francisco Chamber of Commerce Minutes. On June 20, 1916, prior to the formation of the Committee, it was stated:

> The Board [of the Chamber of Commerce] decided to hold a special meeting Wednesday June 21st at 11 a.m. for the purpose of considering action it should take in regard to the present strike situation along the waterfront and the President was authorized to appoint a special committee of three to prepare a draft of resolutions to be considered at that meeting.[6]

Three years and three months later, on October 21, 1919, after the dissolution of the Committee, the Chamber of Commerce Minutes read:

> The President was authorized and requested to appoint a special committee of three to consider the present waterfront situation and what steps might be taken by the Chamber to aid in bringing this strike to a termination as soon as possible.[7]

Thus the work of the Law and Order Committee did not appear to have had any lasting effect. Few of its accomplishments lasted four years. The Committee was the product of hysteria; when it passed, so did the Committee.

---

collapse of the Law and Order Committee. Frederick J. Koster, president of the Chamber of Commerce and chairman of the Law and Order Committee, was also president of the California Barrel Company. Could prohibition have suddenly knocked the bottom out of his business?

Overview

If the word "crusade" could take on a Twentieth Century definition, it would adequately describe the cause of the Law and Order Committee. To the cause of the open shop the Committee was chauvinistic in the purest sense of the word. Quite confident that its cause was righteous, the Committee marched forward into battle, and history, with the confidence of a knight errant. The chronicle is complete and the facts are before the critics. A single fact remains to be revealed; was the Law and Order Committee of the San Francisco Chamber of Commerce a committee of vigilance?

In 1916 the business community of San Francisco was in desperate need of a focal organization. The Chamber of Commerce supplied that commodity. A unifying factor was needed to weld the business community behind the organization. The Waterfront strike proved to be the catalyst. For longevity the support of the general public was essential. The Preparedness Day bombing provided it. The Law and Order Committee was the right organization at the right time in the right place with the right program. It was *the* representative of "organized business" as opposed to "organized labor."

Then the situation turned sour. Rather than mediate and push for rapid settlements, the Committee began to press for an open shop. Then the pressure was applied to achieve a city-wide open shop. As 1916 progressed, the campaign of the Law and Order Committee began to expand into the trials of William McDevitt, Tom Mooney and Warren Billings. As the size and prestige of the Committee increased so did its ambition. By January of 1917 the Committee had completed the bulk of its constructive work but it had had little effect on the industrial conditions of San Francisco. On the state level, the Law and Order program had met with defeat, and worse yet, embarrassment.

The Law and Order Committee was also enigmatic. Unfortunately, from its point of view, it was historically late. Vigilante committees are usually the product of a frontier town where there is no law at all. But by 1916 San Francisco had a duly constituted police and court system which were acknowledged as the representation of the city, county, state and Federal institutions of San Francisco,

California and the United States of America. The conspicuous breaking of the law so characteristic of the earlier vigilante groups was not present, but the more insidious forms of extralegal shenanigans had taken its place. These acts were just as illegal but had more of the trappings of legality. But the distinctions between what was legal and what was not were blurred to the eyes of the citizens and the courts.

At the same time the Law and Order Committee was premature. Had it been able to survive as a viable organization until the end of 1919, it would have found a slot in the era of the Great Red Scare. Radicalism was a suspect philosophy in those days and the anti-Anarchist, antiunion philosophy of the Committee would have had a wholesome ring to the ears of the American public. But by 1919 the Law and Order Committee had been absorbed back into the Chamber of Commerce.

One facet of the Law and Order era that will undoubtedly lead to much speculation is the fact that the Law and Order Committee kept no membership lists. Except for the occasional mention in a newspaper, transcript or courtroom, no lists are available as to the total membership of the Committee. The original five are, of course, bonafide members. But who are the others? The Committee believed that it represented the business community of San Francisco and evidence leads us to assume that in 1916 this was a valid assumption. More specifically, the base of support of the Law and Order Committee was the San Francisco Chamber of Commerce. The Chamber of Commerce was the membership of the Committee. It was the money and membership of the Chamber that gave the Committee the necessary ingredients to begin and carry out its program. It was the Chamber of Commerce which had gone on record in support of the Law and Order Committee. It was also the Chamber of Commerce which had the power to dissolve the Law and Order Committee. Because it did not absorb the Committee until 1919 is proof that the Chamber did not object to the policy of the Committee. Only once did some members attempt to condemn the Committee but they represented only 6 percent of the Chamber's numbers.[1] On the other hand, the membership drive of the Chamber showed that the Law and Order program was being well received by the smaller businessmen throughout the city. It would be hard to believe that someone opposed to the open shop campaign would join the Chamber of Commerce at the height of such a drive.

The Committee of One Hundred can also be considered as

members of the Law and Order Committee. They went on record, in writing, in favor of the Law and Order Committee and campaign. With the exception of Dutton it does not appear that any of the other members of that Committee of One Hundred resigned, protested their appointment or made any attempt to dissociate themselves from the Law and Order Committee. On the contrary, they went on the record as supporting the Law and Order Committee for a period of two years.

The last and most important question to be resolved is, was the Law and Order Committee of the San Francisco Chamber of Commerce a committee of vigilance? More specifically, did the Committee break the law? The answer to this question is probably yes. Below are listed six instances where it is likely the law was broken.

1. One of the cornerstones of the Law and Order program involved the "maintenance of law and order." To this end the Law and Order Committee hired armed guards to patrol the waterfront. In the process of these patrols incidents of violence, and in at least one case, death, were the result. A court could have prosecuted the Law and Order Committee on a charge of counseling or instructing their employees to break the law or incite to riot.

2. In the case of the American Stevedore Company and the control of the drayage companies, the Committee would be in violation of the Sherman Anti-Trust Act. The Law and Order Committee would be considered a trust since it controlled 100 percent of the organized, nonunion labor in the city of San Francisco. Moreover, this labor had been transported across a state line. Secondly, the Law and Order Committee controlled 90 percent of the drayage network in San Francisco which carried goods which had crossed state lines.

3. In the police courts the attorney for the Law and Order Committee framed a striker. The attorney was sent to the courts with the specific assignment to "look into the police courts."[3] The court could have looked upon this as an insinuation to break the law in order to insure conviction.

4. In the Structural Steel strike, the Law and Order Committee was involved with another violation of the Sherman Anti-Trust Act. If what the four firms stated in 1920 was true—that materials would be sidetracked and delayed, that banks would call in loans and that companies which refused to sign with the unions would be driven out of business—then the Committee would have been guilty of collusion to form a Trust. And again the Law and Order Committee

would have been guilty of the hiring of armed guards to break the law in the enforcement of the open shop. A misdemeanor in this strike would have been trespassing and ignoring orders to leave the property.

5. That the Law and Order Committee was a close associate of the district attorney in the Mooney–Billings case cannot be disputed. That the trial of Tom Mooney and Warren Billings was a frame-up cannot be disputed. But it is clear that the Law and Order Committee was involved with the prosecution of Mooney and Billings on more than just an "interested" basis. Since the trial, two Federal investigations, the Densmore Report and the Wickersham Report, have stated unequivocally that the trials of the union men were somewhat less than legal. The Law and Order Committee's close association with Fickert could well be considered aiding and abetting a criminal act, obstruction of justice and denying Tom Mooney and Warren Billings their right to a fair trial under the Fifth Amendment of the United States Constitution.

6. But it is the trial of William McDevitt which will carry the most weight. McDevitt's trial was illegal. Although a mayor may hold a hearing concerning the ability of some member of the civic establishment, it is clearly in violation of the law to place a member of the community on trial *before the mayor* of a city. The trial of William McDevitt was a trial since all parties at the fiasco recognized it as a trial and the records were entered into the archives as a trial. McDevitt's trial was brief, short and done without delay. It was also held — and proceeded — without formality. Above and beyond all other evidence it is the trial of William McDevitt which solidly places the Law and Order Committee into the annals of the Committees of Vigilance of San Francisco.

But perhaps the most unusual ramification of the Law and Order Committee was that it represented the transition in the mentality from the nineteenth to the twentieth century. Vigilantism in the 1800's was to simply hang a man and be done with it. In the 1900's the illegalities had become so blurred with legal phraseology that the thin line between what was legal and what was not was virtually eliminated. The Law and Order, because of its constituents, was allowed to push the limits of the law with absolute impunity. It was an age of behind-the-scenes pressure, flexing of corporate muscle and dark insinuations of commercial complications. This was the new vigilantism, illegal but so "ify" that it will take legal historians to sort through the webs of conspiracy.

Appendix I: Letter, Rolph–Koster

San Francisco, July 10, 1916

To:

MR. FREDERICK J. KOSTER
President,
San Francisco Chamber of Commerce
San Francisco, California

Dear Sir:
Your communication of July 6th, 1916, addressed to the merchants of San Francisco urging them to attend at meeting to be held in the Chamber of Commerce on July 10th, at three P.M., has been received by my office and referred to me.

With due respect to you, I am answering your communication, as a member of the Chamber of Commerce. It has been my purpose to attend your meeting this afternoon, and take with me the rest of the Board of Police Commission and the Chief of Police when I read in the press (about the circulars that were addressed to the merchants of San Francisco).

I regret to differ from those who have advocated and brought about this meeting. In doing so, I am glad to concede the honesty of those, opposed to my views, but I differ from their judgement.

I cannot see wherein a meeting, such as has been invited by your letter, can be of possible good: I do perceive wherein it may do much harm.

The Chamber of Commerce has declared, in a communication, given great publicity in the Press, for the "Open Shop."

This is a general issue which looms large in industrial America.

While conceding the ability and importance and numbers of those who contend for the "open shop", my faith has always been in "Organized Union Labor"!

It is my profound conviction that the union of labor makes for the moral uplift of the country as a whole and places the prosperity of all on a firm basis. The system of collective bargaining is the essence of commercial progress. It protects the laborer and gives solidity to the contract that Capital is able to make with Labor.

While advancing these statements, I am not unmindful of the charge that is brought by the merchants of San Francisco against the Stevedores Union — that it violated it's contract in declaring a strike without sixty days' notice.

I can assure yourself and the members of the Chamber of Commerce that the most influential and experienced labor leaders of San Francisco have expressed to me, their deep regret at this violation of what they consider as a fundamental principle of Unionism. They have felt, and have not hesitated to so state, that the existence of Unionism depends upon its capacity to contract, and its good faith in upholding the contracts when made.

I know, personally, that the influence of the Labor Leaders, generally, has been exerted, unremittingly, to bring about a settlement of the conditions, on the Water Front, produced by this Strike. I am quite sure that, very shortly, the efforts of these Labor Leaders will be crowned with success.

The Strike on the Water Front is a local condition: the announcement of the Chamber of Commerce for the "Open Shop" is a challenge to labor, generally. Naturally, any declaration of hostility to organized Labor weakens the influence of the merchants of the City in dealing with any particular labor dispute.

I do not assume that the merchants of San Francisco, as a whole, are behind any propaganda of hostility to organized Labor. I know the contrary.

I, therefore, fear that a mass meeting, such as has been planned by you, might be misunderstood or misconstrued by Labor and have a tendency to disturb labor conditions in this City.

I believe that both parties to the present controversy should avoid anything likely to increase the disturbance or to arouse bitterness, and should immediately meet with each other for a discussion with a view to adjust their present differences.

When a mass meeting is called, things are often said which were better left unsaid: which are afterwards regretted, but cannot be withdrawn, and which intensify ill-feeling.

The Golden Rule is what is needed in San Francisco, to-day.

Now, Mr. Koster, in concluding this letter, let me add a few remarks as Mayor:

As Chief Executive of this City, I represent the great neutral forces whose concern is that law and order be observed.

Since these troubles have appeared on the Water Front, the Police Department of San Francisco has done its full duty. As long as I am Mayor, the Police Department will impartially enforce the law. That it has done so, is proved by the fact that there has been less violence — less disturbances of the peace — in this Strike than during any similar event in the City's experience.

Respectfully,
[James R. Rolph]

Appendix II:
The Committee of One Hundred

Rabbi Martin A. Meyer
Rev. W.K. Guthrie
F.W. Van Sicklen
Bishop W.F. Nichols
Herbert Fleischhacker
Louis F. Monteagle
K.R. Kingsbury
Bernard Faymonville
H.U. Brandenstein
Frank B. Anderson
Capt. A.E. Anderson
A.B.C. Dohrmann
Allen L. Chickering
Capt. A.E. Payson
Garret McEnerney
Capt. Robert Dollar
George F. Volkman
Jesse W. Lilienthal
John A. McGregor
William T. Sesnon
Lawrence W. Harris
F.L. Washburn
J.D. Spreckles
Selah Chamberlain
B.F. Schlesinger
Capt. Wm. Matson
William H. Hammer
L.B. McMurtry
Jos. D. Grant
S.B. McNear
E.J. Dupue
Wm. H. George
P.S. Teller

Sam G. Buckbee
D. Ghirardelli
A.P. Giannini
George Tourney
I.W. Hellman, Jr.
E.W. Hopkins
R.I. Bentley
Sig. Stern
George Q. Chase
James K. Lynch
H.J. Harbour
Louis Sloss
W.H. Metson
W.H. Wiel
Lester Morse
Leopold Michaels
Wm. J. Dutton
R.M. Hotaling
A.T. DeForrest
Walton N. Moore
Bert S. Hubbard
Andrew Carrigan
Jos. W. Hotchkiss
W. Mayo Newhall
Henry T. Scott
John A. Hooper
Rev. E.J. Hanna
A.K. Munson
Rolla V. Watt
J.K. Armsby
M.A. Gunst
Wm. Sproule
Chas. M. Levy

Gavin McNab
Roy Bishop
R.M. Tobin
Wm. H. Crocker
A.C. Kains
C.O.G. Miller
Fred S. Moody
Frank I. Turner
Max Schmidt
James Tyson
Oscar Sutro
C.C. Moore
Max J. Kuhl
W.B. Wellman
Charles Carpy
Grant Fee
John S. Drum
Constant Meese
John A. Britton
A.C. Christenson
John H. Rosseter
Fred W. Bradley
Frederick E. Magee
R.E. Miller
Warren D. Clark
George A. Pope
Wm. H. Humphrey
A.B. Hammond
W.W. Morrow
Chas. K. Field
Atholl McBean
W.H. Hannam

Appendix III:
Delegates, September 19, 1917, Meeting

Organizations and number of delegates:

Steamboat Owners' Association 5
Motor Car Dealers' Association 8
San Francisco Restaurant Association 7
San Francisco Real Estate Board 7
Wholesale Grocers' Association 6
San Francisco Advertising Club 6
Retail Lumber Dealers' Association 7
Home Industry League of California 6
Board of Trade of San Francisco 6
Rotary Club 5
Franklin Printing Trades Association 6
San Francisco Commercial Club 6
San Francisco Chamber of Commerce 5
Building Industry Association 2
Retail Dry Goods Association of San Francisco 2
San Francisco Automobile Trade Association 5
General Contractors Association 6
Building Material Dealers' Association 6

Total number of delegates 102

Appendix IV:
Top Contributors to Committee

Santa Fe and Southern Pacific	$30,000
San Francisco Chamber of Commerce	$27,000
Bank of California	$25,000
Standard Oil Company	$25,000
California and Hawaiian Sugar Mfg. Co.	$25,000
Emporium	$25,000
Hawaiian Commercial & Sugar Co.	$15,000
Pacific Improvement Company	$10,000
First National Bank	$10,000
Wells Fargo Nevada National Bank	$10,000
Shell Company	$10,000
John Lawson	$10,000
California Barrel Company	$10,000
Moore Watson Dry Goods Company	$10,000
Fireman's Fund Insurance	$10,000
California Fruit Canners' Association	$10,000
W.R. Grace & Company	$10,000
Welch Company	$10,000
Hackfeld Company	$10,000
Matson Navigation Company	$10,000
Alexander & Baldwin	$10,000
Alaska Packers' Association	$10,000
Total contributions	$322,000

Appendix V: Resignations and Cancellations from Chamber of Commerce, 1915-1917

January 1915	38	July 1915	0
February	0	August	50
March	59	September	0
April	19	October	16
May	0	November	10
June	0	December	15
Six month total	116	Six month total	91
		Total for 1915	207
January 1916	31	July 1916	28
February	0	August	5
March	8	September	9
April	43	October	3
May	17	November	4
June	0	December	38
Six month total	99	Six month total	87
		Total for 1916	186
January 1917	38	July 1917	7
February	63	August	43
March	102	September	38
April	154	October	*
May	70	November	*
June	31	December	*
Six month total	458	Six month total	88
		Total for 1917	546

*Unlisted

Chapter Notes

Introduction

[1]"Saxbe Warns of Vigilante Threat," *Los Angeles Times*, September 11, 1974, p. 1.

[2]Herbert Asbury, *The Barbary Coast: An Informal History of the San Francisco Underworld* (New York: Capricorn Books, 1933), pp. 150–64.

[3]Miner Chipman, *Report of Five Months Survey to Law and Order Committee San Francisco Chamber of Commerce, 1917*, unpublished report in the possession of the Library of Industrial Relations at the John F. Kennedy School of Government, Harvard University, p. 33; this is the only source the author could find on the title "gentleman thug."

[4]The best sources for information on the trials of Thomas Mooney and Warren K. Billings are Curt Gentry's *Frame-Up: The Incredible Case of Tom Mooney and Warren Billings* (New York: W.W. Norton, 1967) and Richard H. Frost's *The Mooney Case* (Stanford, Calif., Stanford University Press, 1968).

[5]The best source for the Great Graft Trials is Walton Bean's *Boss Ruef's San Francisco: The Story of the Union Labor Party, Big Business, and the Graft Prosecutions* (Berkeley: University of California Press, 1952.)

Background

[1]Robert Edward Lee Knight, *Industrial Relations in the San Francisco Bay Area, 1900–1918* (Berkeley: University of California Press, 1969), pp. 290–91.

[2]Knight, p. 294; *Labor Clarion*, January 1, 1915.

The Economic Vise

[1]"San Francisco Labor Council has Enviable Record," San Francisco *Chronicle*, February 4, 1917, p. 58; "Building Trades Council of San Francisco is Strong Body: It is most Powerful Organization of its Kind in America," San Francisco *Chronicle*, February 11, 1917, p. 60.

[2]"Industrial Unrest," *Transactions of the Commonwealth Club of California* (San Francisco: 1917), pp. 495–96, 518–20; Robert A. Sayre, *Consumers' Prices: 1914–1918* (New York: National Industrial Conference Board, 1948), pp. 35–41; Frederick L. Ryan, *Industrial Relations in the San Francisco Building Trades* (Norman: University of Oklahoma Press, 1936), pp. 127–30.

[3]Knight, p. 299.

The Chamber and the Waterfront

[1]Knight, p. 302.

[2]San Francisco Chamber of Commerce, *Law and Order in San Francisco: A Beginning* (San Francisco, 1916), p. 1.

[3]*Ibid.*

⁴Chamber of Commerce, p. 2.
⁵Knight, p. 303.
⁶*Ibid.*; "Strikers Pass on Demand for Lumbermen," San Francisco *Call and Post*, July 22, 1916, p. 3.
⁷Knight, p. 304.
⁸Knight, p. 306; "San Francisco Dock Men Vote Strike End," San Francisco *Bulletin*, July 17, 1916, p. 1.
⁹Minutes, San Francisco Chamber of Commerce, May 16, 1916, in the possession of the California Historical Society Library, San Francisco.
¹⁰Minutes, June 21, 1916.
¹¹*Labor Clarion*, June 22, 1916.
¹²Knight, pp. 304–6; Minutes, June 27, 28, 1916.
¹³John Renner to Mayor James R. Rolph, Jr., July 1, 1916, Rolph Papers, in the possession of the California Historical Society Library.
¹⁴Rolph to Renner, July 6, 1916.
¹⁵Knight, p. 305; Gentry, p. 72.

The Formation of the Law and Order Committee

¹Chamber of Commerce, frontispiece.
²Chamber of Commerce to Rolph, July 10, 1916.
³Knight, p. 309; "Speakers Address the Chamber of Commerce," San Francisco Chamber of Commerce *Activities*, July 13, 1916.
⁴"Law and Order," *Coast Seamen's Journal*, July 12, 1916, p. 6; the exact words used by Dollar are not known. The quote most often used appeared in "Planning Another 11th of November," *The Blast*, August 15, 1916, p. 2. Other alleged quotes may be found in Gentry, p. 73; Ernest Jerome Hopkins, *What Happened in the Mooney Case* (New York: Brewer, Warren & Putnam, 1932), p. 11; "End of the Trail," *Labor Clarion*, January 12, 1917, p. 1.
⁵"Water Front Situation," *Labor Clarion*, July 14, 1916, p. 1.
⁶"President Koster Outlines Purpose of Mass Meeting," San Francisco *Chronicle*, July 11, 1916, p. 2.
⁷"Strange News from Russia," *New Republic*, May 5, 1917, p. 8; Greater San Francisco Chamber of Commerce, Law and Order Papers, File 33, p. 1 in the possession of the California Historical Society Library, San Francisco.
⁸Chamber of Commerce, p. 5.
⁹Chamber of Commerce, p. 18.
¹⁰"E Clampus Vitus Barnstorm Old San Francisco," *Pony Express*, March, 1940, p. 2; "Once Historic Landmark of the Comstock," *Pony Express*, June, 1940, p. 1; "The Great Emma Nevada," *Pony Express*, April, 1941, p. 9; "Hellfire Bill from Gold Hill," *Pony Express*, July, 1945, p. 4.
¹¹Chipman, p. 33; "Freedom?" *Coast Seamen's Journal*, August 20, 1916, p. 6; "Sullivan's Speech Before Mission Promotion Association," San Francisco *Daily News*, October 3, 1917, p. 1.
¹²Knight, p. 312; Frost, p. 58.
¹³"Running Amuck," *Labor Clarion*, August 4, 1916, p. 1.
¹⁴"Koster Speaks to the Rotary Club," San Francisco *Chronicle*, October 4, 1916, p. 12.
¹⁵Chamber of Commerce, p. 19; Gentry, p. 73.
¹⁶"The Open Shop," *Argonaut*, July 15, 1916, p. 33.

Chapter Notes 137

¹⁷"The Open Shop Movement," *Argonaut*, August 12, 1916, p. 33.
¹⁸"The Chamber of Commerce and the Open Shop," *Argonaut*, August 19, 1916, p. 115.
¹⁹"Open Shop—Nonunion Shop," *Coast Seamen's Journal*, July 5, 1916, p. 6.
²⁰"Did It or Will It Reconsider," *Labor Clarion*, August 18, 1916, p. 6.
²¹"War on Labor," *The Blast*, July 15, 1916, p. 6; "Crushed Again," *Labor Clarion*, August 20, 1917, p. 8; "Freedom;" *Coast Seamen's Journal*, August 30, 1916, p. 51; "Putrid Politics," *Labor Clarion*, November 9, 1917, p. 40.
²²"Worshiping the God of Dynamite," *The Blast*, August 15, 1916, p. 2; "Planning Another 11th of November," *The Blast*, August 15, 1916, p. 3.
²³"War on Labor," *The Blast*, July 15, 1916, p. 2.
²⁴"The Hope of the Longshoremen," *The Blast*, July 15, 1916, p. 6.
²⁵"Waterfront Situation," *Labor Clarion*, July 14, 1916, p. 1.
²⁶This quote was found in Frost, p. 59, but investigation of the footnote revealed no such quote in the files cited. This is probably an error in the original printing of *The Mooney Case*.
²⁷Rolph to Koster, July 10, 1916.
²⁸*Ibid*.
²⁹Knight, p. 313; "How It Dominates," *Labor Clarion*, August 18, 1916, p. 6; "Compromise Employers Suggestion," San Francisco *Call and Post*, July 14, 1916, p. 1.
³⁰Knight, p. 313.
³¹"San Francisco Dock Men Vote Strike End," San Francisco *Bulletin*, July 17, 1916, p. 1.
³²"Rivermen of San Francisco Plan for New Strike," San Francisco *Call and Post*, July 19, 1916, p. 1; "Ship Owners Name Chamber of Commerce to Handle Parley," San Francisco *Call and Post*, July 12, 1916, p. 1; "Draymen and Rivermen Back to Work," San Francisco *Call and Post*, July 18, 1916, p. 1; "Arbitration Offered by Rivermen," San Francisco *Call and Post*, July 11, 1916, p. 1.
³³Knight, p. 309.
³⁴Knight, pp. 320-21; "Iron Workers Notified Jobs will be Filled," San Francisco *Chronicle*, July 29, 1916, p. 1.
³⁵"Bubble Bursts," *Labor Clarion*, July 21, 1916, p. 10.

The Radicals

¹Richard Drinnon, *Rebel in Paradise: A Biography of Emma Goldman* (Boston: Beacon Press, 1961), pp. 39-41.
²Leon Wolff, *Lockout: The Story of the Homestead Strike of 1892* (New York: Harper & Row, 1965), p. 140.
³Alexander Berkman, *Prison Memoirs of an Anarchist* (New York: Schocken Books, 1912), pp. 7, 29, 57-59.
⁴Berkman, *Prison Memoirs*, p. 33.
⁵"The Golden Rule," *The Blast*, January 15, 1916, p. 1.
⁶"The Myth of the Press," *The Blast*, January 29, 1916, p. 4.
⁷"Labor Mollusks," *The Blast*, January 29, 1916, p. 5.
⁸"Causes of War," *The Blast*, February 12, 1916, p. 5.
⁹"Labor Preparedness," *The Blast*, March 15, 1916, pp. 2-3.
¹⁰*The Blast*, March 4, 1916, p. 7.
¹¹Frost, p. 14; "Program," *The Revolt*, May 6, 1911, p. 4.
¹²*Trial of William McDevitt Before Hon. James Rolph, Jr., Mayor of San Francisco, August 17, 18, 22, 30, 31, 1916*. Unpublished manuscript of transcripts of the trial in the possession of the California Historical Society Library. For further

138 Chapter Notes

information on this footnote, see Section I, Article II of the Charter of the City and County of San Francisco for 1916.

Public Backing for the Committee

[1] Dr. Paul Roberts to Rolph, July 25, 1916.
[2] Gentry, p. 14.
[3] Gentry, p. 15.
[4] Gentry, p. 14.
[5] "Dynamite Attack on Preparedness Parade Kills 6 and Injures 42," Fresno Morning Republican Daily, July 23, 1916, p. 1.
[6] "Labor Opposes Prepare Parade," San Francisco Bulletin, July 8, 1916, p. 4.
[7] Ibid.
[8] Ed Gammons, "Preparedness—For What?" The Blast, July 15, 1916, p. 3.
[9] "Reflections," The Blast, September 1, 1916, p. 6.
[10] Trial of William McDevitt.
[11] "Silent Protest by Labor Is Advocated," San Francisco Bulletin, July 21, 1916, p. 1.
[12] "Gloating" San Francisco Call and Post, July 25, 1916, p. 6.
[13] "Hearst—The Slanderer," Coast Seamen's Journal, July 26, 1916, p. 6.
[14] James Joll, Anarchists (Boston: Little, Brown, 1964), p. 602; Emma Goldman, Living My Life (New York: Alfred A. Knopf, 1931), p. 577.
[15] Alexander Berkman, "Planning Judicial Murder," Mother Earth, September, 1916, p. 602.
[16] Theodora Pollok, "Will Labor Stand for Another Haymarket?" International Socialist Review, December, 1916, p. 262.
[17] Chamber of Commerce, p. 21; Gentry, p. 100.
[18] Otto Irving Wise, "Cleanse City of Animosity and Let Peace Reign," San Francisco Bulletin, July 27, 1916, p. 2; "Citizens to Speak for Order," San Francisco Bulletin, July 26, 1916, p. 1.
[19] Edward H. Hurlbut, "Mass Meeting Held," San Francisco Call and Post, July 27, 1916, p. 1; Gentry, p. 104. It is interesting to note that Hurlbut was the director of publicity for the Law and Order Committee.
[20] Edward H. Hurlbut, "Shades of Vigilantes in Great Mass Meeting," San Francisco Call and Post, July 27, 1916, p. 1.
[21] Chamber of Commerce, p. 38.
[22] "Plan Big Campaign to Enforce the Law," San Francisco Chronicle, July 28, 1916, p. 1; "Chamber of Commerce Law and Order Committee Gets to Work," San Francisco Chronicle, July 25, 1916, p. 1.
[23] "Mooney's Morbid Move," Labor Clarion, July 21, 1916, p. 8.
[24] Drinnon, p. 178.
[25] Greater San Francisco Chamber of Commerce Papers, p. 6.
[26] "Law and Order Aid Promised Steel Plants," San Francisco Call and Post, August 2, 1916, p. 14; "Culinary Workers on Strike," San Francisco Bulletin, August 1, 1916, p. 1; Argonaut, October 14, 1916, p. 255.
[27] Knight, pp. 314–15.
[28] "Culinary Controversy," Labor Clarion, August 4, 1916, p. 10.
[29] Knight, pp. 314–15; "San Francisco Appetite Fed Despite Strike," San Francisco Chronicle, August 16, 1916, p. 8.
[30] "Strike in San Francisco Cafes Spreads Rapidly," San Francisco Call and Post, Aug. 2, 1916, p. 1; "Protection Is Asked by Cafe Men," San Francisco Call and Post, Aug. 3, 1916, p. 1; "Culinary Controversy," Labor Clarion, Aug. 4, 1916, p. 10.

Chapter Notes 139

³¹"Culinary Controversy," *Labor Clarion*, August 4, 1916, p. 10.
³²Chamber of Commerce, p. 29.
³³"The Hope of the Longshoremen," *The Blast*, July 15, 1916, p. 6.
³⁴"In re Culinary Workers," *Labor Clarion*, August 25, 1916; Frederick W. Ely, "Labor Council Preparing for Open Shop War," San Francisco *Bulletin*, September 9, 1916, p. 4.
³⁵"Law and Order," *Coast Seamen's Journal*, November 1, 1916, p. 11; "Exposed—Law and Order," *Labor Clarion*, October 27, 1916, p. 11.
³⁶"In re Culinary Workers," *Labor Clarion*, August 25, 1916; "Pickets Photographed for Court Evidence," San Francisco *Examiner*, August 18, 1916.
³⁷"Strike Lawyers Ousted," San Francisco *Bulletin*, August 4, 1916, p. 1.
³⁸"Law and Order," *Labor Clarion*, June 1, 1916, p. 11.
³⁹Knight, p. 380.
⁴⁰"Law on Picket Assured Place on Ballot," San Francisco *Call and Post*, August 12, 1916, p. 3; Rolph to San Francisco Chamber of Commerce, San Francisco Labor Council, San Francisco Building Trades Council and San Francisco Waterfront Workers Federation, August 10, 1916, Rolph Papers.
⁴¹Rolph to San Francisco Chamber of Commerce, San Francisco Labor Council, San Francisco Building Trades Council and San Francisco Waterfront Workers Federation, August 10, 1916.
⁴²San Francisco Labor Council to Rolph, August 14, 1916; San Francisco Building Trades Council to Rolph, August 11, 1916; San Francisco Waterfront Workers Federation to Rolph, August 16, 1916.
⁴³San Francisco Chamber of Commerce to Rolph, August 16, 1916; "Chamber of Commerce Refuses to Arbitrate," San Francisco *Chronicle*, August 16, 1916, pp. 1, 3.
⁴⁴*Ibid*.
⁴⁵"Arbitration," *Argonaut*, August 19, 1916, p. 114; "The Chamber and the Open Shop," *Argonaut*, August 19, 1916, p. 115.
⁴⁶William Sproule to Rolph, August 17, 1916; "Head of SP Endorses Work of the Chamber of Commerce," San Francisco *Call and Post*, August 18, 1916, p. 13.
⁴⁷Rolph to San Francisco *Chronicle*, August 20, 1916.
⁴⁸"Archbishop Directs Open Shop Parley," San Francisco *Examiner*, August 18, 1916, p. 7; "Open Shop and Union Men Meet," San Francisco *Bulletin*, August 17, 1916, p. 1.
⁴⁹*Ibid*. It should be noted that at least one source indicates that the actual meeting was held in the Merchants Exchange, the home of the San Francisco Chamber of Commerce.

Charles Evans Hughes in San Francisco

¹*Information Please Almanac*, 1977, p. 555.
²*The CBS News Almanac*, 1976, pp. 134–141; U.S. Bureau of the Census, *Statistical Abstracts of the United States*, 1975, p. 435.
³Roseboom, Eugene H., *A History of Presidential Elections* (New York: Macmillan, 1964), p. 380.
⁴Roseboom, pp. 375–390; Pusey, Merlo J., *Charles Evans Hughes* (New York: Macmillan, 1951), p. 340.
⁵Pusey, p. 340.
⁶Pusey, p. 341; Olin, Spencer C., Jr., *California's Prodigal Sons* (Berkeley: University of California Press, 1968), p. 125.
⁷Pusey, p. 241; Olin, p. 126.

8Olin, p. 130.
9*Ibid.*
10Olin, p. 131; Pusey, pp. 341–43.
11Olin, p. 132; Pusey, pp. 341–43.
12Pusey, p. 343.
13*Ibid.*; Olin, p. 133; "Hughes Talks of National Issues to Large Throng," San Francisco *Bulletin*, August 19, 1916, p. 2.
14Pusey, p. 343.
15Olin, p. 135.
16Pusey, p. 344.
17Olin, p. 135.
18*Ibid.*
19*Ibid.*
20"All Waiters Quit, but the Hughes Luncheon Is Success," San Francisco *Chronicle*, August 20, 1916, p. 3.
21Rudolph Spreckles to James D. Phelan, September 20, 1916, Phelan Papers, quoted by permission of the Bancroft Library, University of California, Berkeley.
22"Hughes Leaves San Francisco with Fall Ballot Won," San Francisco *Chronicle*, August 20, 1916, p. 3.
23"The Commercial Club Strike," *Argonaut*, August 26, 1916, p. 131.
24Pusey, p. 352.
25Pusey, p. 346.
26Knight, p. 316.
27Charles Evans Hughes, *The Autobiographical Notes of Charles Evans Hughes* (Cambridge: Harvard University Press, 1973), p. 182.

The Trial of William McDevitt

1"Forces of Evil," *Argonaut*, July 7, 1917, p. 421.
2"Ministers are Told of Fight for Open Shop," San Francisco *Chronicle*, August 22, 1916, p. 8.
3*Ibid.*
4*Ibid.*
5Asbury, pp. 307–11.
6"Minister Speaks for 8 Hour Day," San Francisco *Call and Post*, August 14, 1916, p. 2.
7"Dutton Given Chamber of Commerce Stand by Pastros," San Francisco *Call and Post*, August 22, 1916, p. 1.
8"Open Shop Fight Subject to Talk," San Francisco *Bulletin*, August 24, 1916, p. 4; "Cafeteria May be Opened by Strikers," San Francisco Bulletin, August 24, 1916, p. 4.
9"Koster Replies to Dr. Dutton's Remark," San Francisco *Call and Post*, August 25, 1916, p. 1.
10*Ibid.*
11"Open Shop Fight Subject to Talk," San Francisco *Bulletin*, August 24, 1916, p. 4.
12"Labor and Clergy to Meet Today," San Francisco *Call and Post*, August 25, 1916, p. 2.
13McDevitt, *passim*.
14"The Open Shop," *Argonaut*, July 15, 1916, p. 33; "Mr. McDevitt's Jocularity Was Not Funny," San Francisco *Call and Post*, August 14, 1916, p. 4; "The Chamber of Commerce and the Open Shop," *Argonaut*, August 19, 1916, p. 115; "McDevitt

Defends Himself," San Francisco *Bulletin*, August 17, 1916, p. 15.
    [15]"Anarchy," *Argonaut*, July 29, 1916, p. 66.
    [16]"Mr. McDevitt's Jocularity Was Not Funny," San Francisco *Call and Post*, August 14, 1916, p. 115.
    [17]"A Call to Mayor Rolph," *Argonaut*, August 5, 1916, p. 81.
    [18]"Fire McDevitt Demand, Rolph Asks Time," San Francisco *Call and Post*, August 2, 1916, p. 1; McDevitt, *passim*.
    [19]McDevitt, pp. 2, 3, 4, 8.
    [20]McDevitt, p. 6.
    [21]McDevitt, p. 8.
    [22]McDevitt, p. 9.
    [23]McDevitt, p. 12.
    [24]McDevitt, p. 15.
    [25]McDevitt, pp. 13, 16, 17.
    [26]McDevitt, pp. 18, 21.
    [27]*Ibid.*; "Law and Order Answered," *Labor Clarion*, August 4, 1916.
    [28]McDevitt, pp. 21, 22.
    [29]McDevitt, p. 23; Rolph to McDevitt, August 11, 1916.
    [30]*Argonaut*, August 19, 1916, p. 115.
    [31]Chamber of Commerce, p. 5; McDevitt, p. 2.
    [32]McDevitt, pp. 26, 27.
    [33]"For the Revolution," *The Revolt*, May 13, 1911, p. 1; "The McDevitt–Goldman Debate," *The Revolt*, May 27, 1911, p. 1.
    [34]McDevitt, p. 28.
    [35]McDevitt, pp. 32, 40–41.
    [36]McDevitt, pp. 34, 35, 36, 37, 40.
    [37]McDevitt, pp. 40–42.
    [38]McDevitt, pp. 45–50, 63.
    [39]McDevitt, pp. 63, 67, 69; "Labor Man Answers Chamber of Commerce," San Francisco *Bulletin*, August 20, 1916, p. 3.
    [40]Chamber of Commerce, frontispiece; McDevitt, pp. 50, 70–72.
    [41]McDevitt, pp. 73, 76, 77. The author could find no such "wandering statements." The transcript might not be complete, Drew might be exaggerating or the author might not have interpreted some of the testimony as "wandering."
    [42]McDevitt, pp. 80, 83.
    [43]McDevitt, pp. 86, 89–96.
    [44]McDevitt, pp. 116, 118.
    [45]McDevitt, pp. 128–29, 130, 132–34.
    [46]"Anarchy," *Argonaut*, July 29, 1916, p. 66.
    [47]McDevitt, pp. 135, 137–39.
    [48]McDevitt, pp. 142–238.
    [49]McDevitt, pp. 245, 249, 553; "Labor Man Answers Chamber of Commerce," San Francisco *Bulletin*, August 17, 1916, p. 15; "McDevitt's Fate Up to Mayor," San Francisco *Bulletin*, August 31, 1916, p. 1.

The Committee vs. the Unions

[1]Knight, p. 320.
    [2]"Open Shop Fight Renewed," *Labor Clarion*, August 25, 1916, p. 16.
    [3]"Dynamite Is Found at Mills," San Francisco *Bulletin*, September 2, 1916, p. 2; "Discover Dynamite in San Francisco Lumberyards," Fresno *Morning Republican Daily*, September 3, 1916, p. 1.

142 Chapter Notes

⁴"Discover Dynamite Plant in Lumber Company Yard," San Francisco *Chronicle*, September 3, 1916, p. 38; "Discover Dynamite in San Francisco Lumber Yards," Fresno *Morning Republican Daily*, September 3, 1916, p. 1.

⁵"The New Strike," *The Blast*, June 1, 1916, p. 5.

⁶"Legal Forces of City Called Out for Mayor's War," San Francisco *Chronicle*, November 29, 1916, p. 5.

⁷Knight, p. 320; Chamber of Commerce, p. 34.

⁸Knight, p. 321.

⁹*Ibid.*

¹⁰"Law and Order Aid Promised Steel Plants," San Francisco *Call and Post*, August 2, 1916, p. 14.

¹¹Pacific Rolling Mill to Rolph, August 16, 1916.

¹²"Suit Bares Rift in Iron Trades Organization," San Francisco *Chronicle*, July 1, 1920, p. 17.

¹³*Ibid.*

¹⁴San Francisco *Bulletin*, October 6, 1916, p. 4; San Francisco *Call and Post*, October 6, 1916, p. 7; *Argonaut*, October 14, 1916, p. 255.

¹⁵*Ibid.*

¹⁶*Ibid.*

¹⁷Dyer Brothers, Golden West Iron Works, Mortenson Construction Company, Pacific Rolling Mill Company, Ralston Iron Works, Schrader Iron Works and Western Iron Works to Rolph, November 14, 1916.

¹⁸*Ibid.*

¹⁹*Ibid.*

²⁰William Michel, to Rolph, November 17, 1916, p. 1.

²¹*Ibid.*

²²*Ibid.*

²³San Francisco Chamber of Commerce *Activities*, July 27, 1916, p. 1.

²⁴"Open Shop is the Slogan of Business Men," San Francisco *Chronicle*, August 29, 1916, p. 3; San Francisco Chamber of Commerce *Activities*, vol. 3, no. 30, p. 1.

²⁵Koster to Rolph, August 23, 1916; "12,000 Get Bid to Join Ranks of Chamber of Commerce," San Francisco *Call and Post*, August 17, 1916, p. 9.

²⁶Koster to Rolph, August 23, 1916.

²⁷"'Open Shop' is the Slogan of Businessmen," San Francisco *Chronicle*, August 29, 1916, p. 3; "Chamber of Commerce Campaign Closes with 7282 Members," San Francisco *Chronicle*, September 2, 1916, p. 8.

²⁸"Legal Forces of City Called Out for Mayor's War," San Francisco *Chronicle*, November 29, 1916, p. 5.

²⁹*Ibid.*; "Buzzards of Our City," *Labor Clarion*, December 8, 1916, p. 1.

³⁰"Legal Forces of City Called Out for Mayor's War," San Francisco *Chronicle*, November 29, 1916, p. 5.

³¹"Buzzards of Our City," *Labor Clarion*, December 8, 1916, p. 1.

³²"Labor War Waged at Hospital," San Francisco *Bulletin*, November 27, 1916, p. 1.

³³"Buzzards of Our City," *Labor Clarion*, December 8, 1916, p. 1; "Contractor and Men Taken off Job by Force," San Francisco *Bulletin*, November 29, 1916, p. 1.

³⁴"Reardon to Stop Work on Hospital," San Francisco *Bulletin*, November 29, 1916, p. 1.; "Mayor Rolph Acts," *Labor Clarion*, December 1, 1916, p. 6.

³⁵"Mayor Rolph Acts," *Labor Clarion*, December 1, 1916, p. 6; "Reardon to Stop Work on Hospital," San Francisco *Bulletin*, November 29, 1916, p. 1; Rolph to San Francisco City Attorney, December 28, 1916; San Francisco Department of Public Works to Rolph, December 29, 1916.

³⁶"Buzzards of Our City," *Labor Clarion*, December 8, 1916, p. 1.

37San Francisco Board of Election Commissioners, "Proposed Ordinances and Charter Amendments to Be Submitted November 7, 1916," p. 1.
38San Francisco Chamber of Commerce *Activities*, September 28, 1916, p. 1.
39"Anti-Picketing Law Favored by the Chamber of Commerce," San Francisco *Bulletin*, November 2, 1916, p. 8; "'Picketing' In Its Essence," *Argonaut*, August 19, 1916, p. 113.
40Frederick J. Koster, "Law and Order in San Francisco," unpublished speech to the San Francisco Chamber of Commerce, February, 1918, in the possession of the California Historical Society Library.
41Knight, pp. 313, 318–19; Chamber of Commerce, foreword, San Francisco Chamber of Commerce *Activities*, Vol. 3, Issue 43, pp. 6–9; "San Francisco Complete Ballot on Amendments," San Francisco *Chronicle*, November 10, 1916, p. 1.
42Knight, pp. 313, 318–19.
43Chamber of Commerce, pp. 30–33.

"The End of the Trail"

1Chamber of Commerce.
2"Reflections: The Scab Book," *The Blast*, January 15, 1917, p. 5; "The End of the Trail," *Labor Clarion*, January 12, 1917, p. 1.
3"The End of the Trail," *Labor Clarion*, January 12, 1917, p. 1.
4*Ibid.*
5*Ibid.*
6"Crushed Again," *Labor Clarion*, April 20, 1917, p. 8.
7*Ibid.*
8*Ibid.*
9*Ibid.*; "Making Strikes Illegal," *Coast Seamen's Journal*, January 31, 1917, p. 6.
10"Crushed Again," *Labor Clarion*, April 20, 1917, p. 8; "Chamber of Commer-Bill Beaten in Committee," San Francisco *Bulletin*, March 23, 1917, p. 9.
11Knight, p. 319.
12"50 Cars Tied Up at Haight & Market," San Francisco *Chronicle*, August 12, 1917, p. 1; "Mayor Is Not Ready to Buy United Railroads," San Francisco *Bulletin*, November 2, 1917, p. 10.
13"Koster Demands Stop Be Put to Strike Violence," San Francisco *Chronicle*, August 25, 1917, p. 2; "Such Acts Denounced as Crime by Rolph," San Francisco *Call and Post*, September 8, 1917, p. 3.
14San Francisco *Bulletin*, August 25, 1917, p. 3.
15"The Mayor and the Strike," *Argonaut*, September 15, 1917, pp. 161–62.
16"The Real Issues," *Argonaut*, August 25, 1917, p. 113.
17"You Still Believe in Grapeshot; Says Rolph to Koster," San Francisco *Chronicle*, August 25, 1917, p. 2.
18Knight, p. 346.
19"The Car Strike and the Mayor," *Argonaut*, September 27, 1916, p. 177.
20"URR Strike," *Argonaut*, September 22, 1917, p. 177.
21"Sullivan's Speech Before Mission Promotion Association," San Francisco *Daily News*, October 3, 1917, p. 1.
22San Francisco Chamber of Commerce *Activities*, Sept. 27, 1917, pp. 231, 236.
23"Sullivan's Speech Before Mission Promotion Association," San Francisco *Daily News*, October 3, 1917, p. 1.
24"URR Officials Confident," San Francisco *Chronicle*, August 13, 1917, p. 2; "200 More Now Enroute from New York," San Francisco *Chronicle*, August 19, 1917, p. 1.

144 Chapter Notes

²⁵Gentry, pp. 196, 214, 221; "Backfire in the Bomb Case," *Argonaut*, May 5, 1917, p. 275; "Clarke to Conduct Oxman Hearing," San Francisco *Chronicle*, April 28, 1917, p. 1; "Chamber of Commerce Attorney to Aid Fickert in Bomb Trials," San Francisco *Chronicle*, April 29, 1917, p. 1.
²⁶Gentry, p. 223.
²⁷"Fickert Recall," *Argonaut*, November 24, 1917, p. 320.
²⁸San Francisco Chamber of Commerce *Activities*, vol. 4, no. 50, p. 320.
²⁹"Fickert Draws Commendation of Roosevelt," San Francisco *Chronicle*, November 18, 1917, p. 1.
³⁰Fremont Older to R.A. Crothers, July 16, 1918, Older Papers, quoted by permission of The Bancroft Library, University of California, Berkeley.
³¹"The Bulletin," *Argonaut*, August 10, 1918, p. 81; Gentry, p. 253.
³²Lewis Francis Byington, *The History of San Francisco* (Chicago: S.J. Clarke Pub. Co., 1931), pp. 18–22; Minutes, August 20, 1919.

The Civic Reaction to the Committee

¹"Mayor Is Not Ready to Buy United Railroads," San Francisco *Bulletin*, November 2, 1917, p. 10.
²"Public Works Board Flayed by Supervisors," San Francisco *Chronicle*, February 4, 1919, p. 8.
³Gentry, p. 351; "Chamber of Commerce Silent on Rolph Labor Day Address," San Francisco *Call and Post*, September 5, 1916, p. 7.
⁴*Ibid*.
⁵"A Time for Caution," *Labor Clarion*, December 7, 1917, p. 8.
⁶Alexander Berkman, "Back in New York," *Mother Earth*, November, 1916, pp. 668–69.
⁷Alexander Berkman, "The Life and Death Struggle in San Francisco," *Mother Earth*, December, 1916, p. 698.
⁸Robert Minor, "The San Francisco Bomb," *Mother Earth*, September, 1916, p. 609.
⁹Eugene V. Debs, "Tom Mooney Sentenced to Death," *International Socialist Review*, April, 1917, pp. 613–14.
¹⁰Chamber of Commerce, p. 18; Minutes, September 26, 1916.
¹¹"Open Shop Subject to Fight," San Francisco *Bulletin*, August 24, 1916, p. 4.
¹²Minutes, December, 1914 to December, 1917.
¹³Dr. B.M. Rastall, "Industrial Survey," *Organized Labor*, January 27, 1917; "Rolph and the 'Law and Order' Committee," San Francisco *Bulletin*, October 3, 1917; "Sullivan's Speech Before Mission Promotion Association," San Francisco *Daily News*, October 3, 1917, p. 1.
¹⁴Chipman, *passim*.
¹⁵Chipman, pp. 7, 35, 39.
¹⁶Hubert Howe Bancroft, *Modern Fallacies: An Added Chapter to "Retrospection"* (New York: Bancroft, 1915), p. 28.
¹⁷Alexander Berkman, "Planning Judicial Murder," *Mother Earth*, September, 1916, p. 599.
¹⁸Chipman, p. 41.
¹⁹Chipman, pp. 47–49.
²⁰"Bankers Clash Over Chamber of Commerce Donation," San Francisco *Call and Post*, July 27, 1916, p. 6.
²¹Chipman, p. 64.
²²Chipman, pp. 2, 11–19, 23, 26, 29, 63.

[23]"Critics Assail Character of San Francisco Chamber," San Francisco *Chronicle*, March 4, 1919, p. 4. Repeated efforts by the author to contact the Civic League of Improvement Clubs and Associations in San Francisco have not been successful.
[24]League of Women Voters Papers, May 11, 1917, *passim*, in the possession of the California Historical Society Library. San Francisco *Chronicle*, April 30, 1917.
[25]Bureau of Municipal Research, New York, *Report on a Survey of the Government of the City and County of San Francisco Prepared for the San Francisco Real Estate Board* (San Francisco, 1916), p. 185.
[26]"Chamber of Commerce Attorney to Aid Fickert in Bomb Trials," San Francisco *Chronicle*, April 29, 1917, p. 1; "Chamber of Commerce is Starting Campaign to Settle Strike on Front," San Francisco *Chronicle*, July 12, 1916, p. 1.

The Demise of the Committee

[1]San Francisco Chamber of Commerce, "The Golden Gate," May 12, 1920, p. 4; Chamber of Commerce, p. 12; "Congratulations to Seattle," *Argonaut*, March 31, 1917, p. 193; "San Francisco 1916 Foreign Trade Record Breaking: Exports Quadrupuled," San Francisco *Call and Post*, December 27, 1916, p. 1; "San Francisco Capital Invested," San Francisco *Chronicle*, December 27, 1916, p. 1; "San Francisco Growth as Figures Show It," San Francisco *Chronicle*, January 17, 1917, p. 8.
[2]Knight, p. 338; "The Bay of San Francisco," *Argonaut*, December 12, 1917, p. 7; "Twenty-Five Million to Improve Shipyards," San Francisco *Chronicle*, November 23, 1916, p. 3; "Six Torpedo Boats for Navy Department," San Francisco *Chronicle*, November 19, 1916, p. 1; "San Francisco Leads Coast in Shipbuilding," San Francisco *Chronicle*, December 22, 1916, p. 6; "Millions to Extend City's Factory Zone," San Francisco *Chronicle*, February 8, 1917, p. 9; "San Francisco Picked as Fleet Base for Navy," San Francisco *Chronicle*, November 23, 1916, p. 3; "San Francisco Launches Navy Base Campaign," San Francisco *Chronicle*, November 11, 1916, p. 11; "Union Iron Works Gets $7,130,000 Navy Award," San Francisco *Chronicle*, November 19, 1916, p. 1; "San Francisco Excels Any Two Other Cities," San Francisco *Chronicle*, January 3, 1917, p. 3.
[3]Knight, pp. 335, 380; "Strange News from Russia," *New Republic*, May 5, 1917, p. 8.
[4]Knight, p. 320.
[5]Minutes, October 23, 1917, October 8, 1918, March 11, 1919, May 20, 1919; "Chamber of Commerce Plans to Intervene in Dock Strike," San Francisco *Chronicle*, October 29, 1919, p. 4.
[6]Minutes, June 20, 1916.
[7]Minutes, October 21, 1919.

Overview

[1]"Open Shop Subject to Fight," San Francisco *Bulletin*, August 24, 1916, p. 4.
[2]Chamber of Commerce, p. 5.
[3]"Strike Lawyers Ousted," San Francisco *Bulletin*, August 4, 1916, p. 1; "Law and Order," *Labor Clarion*, June 1, 1916, p. 11; "Chamber of Commerce Attorney to Aid Fickert in Bomb Trials," San Francisco *Chronicle*, April 29, 1917, p. 1; "Chamber of Commerce Is Starting Campaign to Settle Strike on Front," San Francisco *Chronicle*, July 12, 1916, p. 1.

Bibliography

Secondary Sources

Asbury, Herbert. *The Barbary Coast: An Informal History of the San Francisco Underworld.* New York: Capricorn Books, 1933.
Allen, Frederick Lewis. *Only Yesterday: An Informal History of the Twenties.* New York: Harper & Row, 1931.
Bancroft, Hubert Howe. *Modern Fallacies: An Added Chapter to Retrospection.* New York: Bancroft, 1915.
Barck, Oscar Theodore, Jr., and Nelson Manfred Blake. *Since 1900: A History of the United States in Our Times.* New York: Macmillan, 1965.
Bean, Walton. *Boss Ruef's San Francisco: The Story of the Union Labor Party, Big Business, and the Graft Prosecutions.* Berkeley: University of California Press, 1952.
_____. *California: An Interpretive History.* New York: McGraw-Hill, 1968.
Berkman, Alexander. *The Bolshevik Myth.* London: Hutchinson, 1925.
_____. *Prison Memoirs of an Anarchist.* New York: Schocken Books, 1912.
Bing, Alexander M. *War-Time Strikes and their Adjustment.* New York: E.P. Dutton, 1921.
Brissenden, Paul Frederick, *The IWW: A Study of American Syndicalism.* London: P.S. King & Sons, 1920.
Bruce, John. *Gaudy Century: The Story of San Francisco's 100 Years of Robust Journalism.* New York: Random House, 1948.
Burke, Robert E. *Olson's New Deal for California.* Berkeley: University of California Press, 1953.
Byington, Lewis Francis, and Oscar Lewis, eds. *The History of San Fransico.* Chicago: S.J. Clarke Pub. Co., 1931.
Caughey, John Walton. *California.* Englewood Cliffs, N.J.: Prentice-Hall, 1931.
Chafee, Zechariah, Jr. *Freedom of Speech.* New York: Harcourt, Brace & Company, 1920.
Christoph, James Bernard. "Alexander Berkman and American Anarchism." Unpublished master's thesis, University of Minnesota, 1952.
Cleland, Robert Glass. *California in our Time: 1900-1940.* New York: Alfred A. Knopf, 1947.
Conlin, Joseph R., ed. *The American Radical Press, 1880-1960.* Westport, Conn.: Greenwood Press, 1974.
Coy, Owen C. *Guide to the County Archives of California.* Sacramento: California Historical Survey Commission, 1919.
Creel, George. *Rebel at Large: Recollections of 50 Crowded Years.* New York: G.P. Putnam's Sons, 1947.

Cross, Ira B. *A History of the Labor Movement in California*. Berkeley: University of California Press, 1935.

DeFord, Miriam Allen. "California's Disgrace: How and Why Tom Mooney Was Framed, Including a Complete History of the World Famous Mooney Case from 1916 to 1938." Unpublished manuscript in the possession of the Bancroft Library, University of California, Berkeley, 1938.

Delmatier, McIntosh and Waters, eds. *The Rumble of Calfornia Politics*. New York: Wiley, 1970.

Dowell, Eldridge Foster. *A History of Criminal Syndicalism Legislation in the United States*. Baltimore: Johns Hopkins Press, 1939.

Drinnon, Richard. *Rebel in Paradise: A Biography of Emma Goldman*. Boston: Beacon Press, 1961.

———, and Anna Marie Drinnon, eds. *Nowhere at Home: Emma Goldman and Alexander Berkman*. New York: Schocken Books, 1975.

Dubofsky, Melvyn. *We Shall Be All: A History of the Industrial Workers of the World*. Chicago: Quadrangle Books, 1969.

Duffus, Robert L. *The Tower of Jewels: Memoirs of San Francisco*. New York: W.W. Norton, 1960.

Francis, Robert Coleman. "A History of Labor on the San Francisco Waterfront." Unpublished doctoral dissertation, University of California, Berkeley, 1934.

Frost, Richard H. *The Mooney Case*. Stanford, Calif.: Stanford University Press, 1968.

Gentry, Curt. *Frame-Up: The Incredible Case of Tom Mooney and Warren Billings*. New York: W.W. Norton, 1967.

Goldman, Emma. *Anarchism: What It Really Stands For*. New York: Mother Earth Pub. Co., 1916.

———. *Living My Life*. New York: Alfred A. Knopf, 1931.

———. *My Disillusionment in Russia*. London: C.W. Daniels Co., 1925.

Goldman, Eric F. *Rendezvous with Destiny: A History of Modern American Reform*. New York: Random House, 1955.

Hamner, Philip M., ed. *A Guide to Archives and Manuscripts in the United States*. New Haven, Conn.: Yale University Press, 1961.

Harbaugh, William Henry. *Power and Responsibility: Life and Times of Theodore Roosevelt*. New York: Farrar, Straus & Cudahy, 1961.

Hoffman, Robert, ed. *Anarchism*. New York: Atherton Press, 1970.

Holmes, Oliver Wendell. "The Standard of the Clear and Present Danger." *Loyalty in a Democratic State*, ed. by John C. Wahlke. Lexington: D.C. Heath, 1952.

Hopkins, Ernest Jerome. *What Happened in the Mooney Case*. New York: Brewer, Warren & Putnam, 1932.

Howell, Peter D. "The IWW and the Espionage Act: The Roots of the California Trail." Unpublished master's thesis, San Jose State College, 1969.

Hughes, Charles Evans. *The Autobiographical Notes of Charles Evans Hughes*. Cambridge, Mass.: Harvard University Press, 1973.

Jensen, Joan M. *The Price of Vigilance*. Chicago: Rand McNally, 1968.
Joll, James. *Anarchists*. Boston: Little, Brown, 1964.
Knight, Robert Edward Lee. *Industrial Relations in the San Francisco Bay Area: 1900–1918*. Berkeley: University of California Press, 1960.
Kornbluh, Joyce L., ed. *Rebel Voices: An IWW Anthology*. Ann Arbor: University of Michigan Press, 1964.
Lewis, Oscar. *San Francisco: Mission to Metropolis*. Berkeley, Calif.: Howell North Books, 1966.
Link, Arthur S. *Woodrow Wilson and the Progressive Era*. New York: Harper & Bros., 1954.
Lippmann, Walter. *Early Writings*. New York: Liveright, 1970.
London, Jack. *The Iron Heel*. New York: Macmillan, 1934.
Melendy, H. Brett, and Benjamin F. Gilbert. *The Governors of California: Peter H. Burnett to Edmund G. Brown*. Georgetown, Calif.: Talisman Press, 1965.
Millard, Bailey. *History of the San Francisco Bay Region*. Chicago: American Historical Society, 1924.
Moley, Jr., Raymond. *The American Legion Story*. New York: Duell, Sloan and Pearce, 1966.
Mowry, George E. *The California Progressives*. Berkeley: University of California Press, 1951.
Murray, Robert K. *Red Scare: A Study in National Hysteria: 1919–1920*. Minneapolis: University of Minnesota Press, 1955.
O'Connor, Harvey. *Revolution in Seattle*. New York: Monthly Review Press, 1964.
Ohlson, Robert U. "The History of the San Francisco Labor Council." Unpublished master's thesis, University of California, Berkeley, 1941.
Olin, Spencer C., Jr. *California's Prodigal Sons: Hiram Johnson and the Progressives: 1911–1917*. Berkeley: University of California Press, 1968.
Parker, Carleton H. *The Casual Laborer and Other Essays*. New York: Harcourt, Brace & Howe, 1920.
Perlman, Selig, and Philip Taft. *Labor Movements*. Vol. IV of *History of Labor in the United States, 1896–1932*. New York: Macmillan, 1935.
Pomeroy, Earl. *The Pacific Slope: A History of California, Oregon, Washington, Idaho, Utah and Nevada*. New York: Alfred A. Knopf, 1965.
Post, Louis F. *The Deportations Delirium of Nineteen Twenty: A Personal Narrative of an Historical Official Experience*. Chicago: Charles H. Kerr, 1923.
Preston, William, Jr. *Aliens and Dissenters: Federal Suppression of Radicals: 1903–1933*. Cambridge, Mass.: Harvard University Press, 1963.
Pusey, Merlo J. *Charles Evans Hughes*. New York: Macmillan, 1951.
Renshaw, Patrick. *The Wobblies: A Story of Syndicalism in the United States*. Garden City, N.Y.: Doubleday, n.d.
Robinson, Robert M. "A History of the Teamsters in the San Francisco Bay Area: 1850.1950." Unpublished doctoral dissertation, University of California, Berkeley, 1951.
Rocqu, Margaret Miller, ed. *California Local History: A Bibliography*

and Union List of Library Holdings. Stanford, Calif.: Stanford University Press, 1970.
Roseboom, Eugene. A History of Presidential Elections. New York: Macmillan, 1964.
Russell, Francis. The President Makers. Boston: Little, Brown, 1976.
Ryan, Frederick L. Industrial Relations in the San Francisco Building Trades. Norman: University of Oklahoma Press, 1936.
Saposs, David J. Left Wing Unionism: A Study of Radical Policies and Tactics. New York: Russell & Russell, 1926.
Shulman, Alix Kates, ed. Red Emma Speaks. New York: Random House, 1972.
Sinclair, Upton. I, Candidate for Governor: And How I Got Licked. Pasadena: By the Author, 1934.
Slobodek, Mitchell. A Selective Bibliography of California Labor History. Los Angeles: Institute of Indust. Rel., University of California, 1964.
Starr, Todd, and Curti, eds. Living American Documents. New York: Harcourt, Brace & World, 1961.
Stephens, Governor William D. California in the War: War Addresses, Proclamations and Patriotic Messages. Issued by the War History Department of the California Historical Survey Commission, 1919?.
Weintraub, Hyman. "The IWW in California: 1905–1931." Unpublished master's thesis, University of California, Los Angeles, 1947.
Wells, Evelyn. Fremont Older. New York: D. Appleton-Century, 1936.
Wolff, Leon. Lockout: The Story of the Homestead Strike of 1892. New York: Harper & Row, 1965.
Zarchin, Michael M. Glimpses of Jewish Life in San Francisco. Oakland, Calif.: Judah L. Magues Memorial Museum, 1964.

Newspapers and Periodicals

Argonaut
Arizona and the West
Atlantic Monthly
Butler County Press
California Historical Quarterly
Coast Seaman's Journal
Forum
Fresno Morning Republican Daily
International Socialist Review
Journal of the West
Labor Clarion
Labor History
Literary Digest
Los Angeles Times
Main Sheet
Masses
Midstream
Mississippi Valley Historical Review
Mother Earth
Municipal Record
Nation
New Republic
New York Times
Newsweek
Olympian
Organized Labor
Outlook
Pacific Historian
Pacific Historical Review
Pony Express
Revolt
Riverside Press

150 Newspapers and Periodicals

Sacramento *Bee*
San Francisco *Bulletin*
San Francisco *Business*
San Francisco *Call and Post*
San Francisco Chamber of
  Commerce *Activities*
San Francisco *Chronicle*
San Francisco *Examiner*

San Francisco *Examiner*
Southern California Quarterly
Sunset
Survey
The Blast
Time
Upton Sinclair's

Primary Sources

(Those sources listed which are followed by the letters "CHS" are from the California Historical Society Library in San Francisco; "UCB" indicates the University of California at Berkeley.)

Board of Election Commissioners. "Proposed Ordinances and Charter Amendments to Be Submitted November 7, 1916," in the possession of the Sutro Library, University of San Francisco.
Board of Supervisors. "Statements and Arguments." San Francisco, 1916. (CHS)
Bureau of Municipal Research, New York. *Report on a Survey of the Government of the City and County of San Francisco Prepared for the San Francisco Real Estate Board.* San Francisco: Rincon Pub. Co., 1916. (CHS)
Chipman, Miner. *Report of Five Months Survey to Law and Order Committee, San Francisco Chamber of Commerce.* Unpublished survey in the possession of the Library of Industrial Relations, John F. Kennedy School of Government, Harvard University, 1917.
Crocker-Langley's San Francisco *Directory, 1916.* (CHS)
William Denman Papers. (Bancroft Library, UCB)
Duff, Harvey. "The Silent Defenders, Courts and Capitalism in California. A Brief History of the Up Hill Struggle of the IWW in California. An Expose of the Sacramento Frame-Up and Conviction." Chicago: IWW, 1920(?). (CHS)
Greater San Francisco Chamber of Commerce Papers. (CHS)
Francis J. Heney Papers. (Bancroft Library, UCB)
Hichborn, Franklin. "California Politics: 1891–1939." Unpublished manuscript in the possession of the University of Santa Clara, 1951(?).
Koster, Frederick J. "Law and Order in San Francisco." Unpublished speech to the San Francisco Chamber of Commerce, 1918. (CHS)
League of Women Voters, San Francisco, Paper. (Also known as the San Francisco Center.) (CHS)
Minutes. San Francisco Chamber of Commerce. (CHS)
Thomas J. Mooney Papers. (Bancroft Library, UCB)
National Executive Committee of the Socialist Labor Party. "As to Politics: A Discussion upon the Relative Importance of Political Action and of

Class Consciousness Economic Action, and the Urgent Need of Both."
   New York: Socialist Labor Party, 1921. (Bancroft Library, UCB)
John Francis Neylan Papers. (Bancroft Library, UCB)
James D. Phelan Papers. (Bancroft Library, UCB)
James R. Rolph, Jr., Papers. (CHS)
Chester H. Rowell Papers. (Bancroft Library, UCB)
San Francisco Chamber of Commerce. "The Golden Gate." San Francisco:
   San Francisco Chamber of Commerce, 1920. (CHS)
———. "Industrial San Francisco in Word and Picture." San Francisco:
   San Francisco Chamber of Commerce, 1920. (CHS)
———. "Law and Order in San Francisco: A Beginning." San Francisco:
   H.S. Crocker Co., 1916. (CHS)
Transactions of the Commonwealth Club of California.
Trial of William McDevitt Before Hon. James Rolph, Jr., Mayor of San
   Francisco, August 17, 18, 22, 30, 31, 1916. Unpublished manuscript.
   (CHS)
John Downey Works Papers. (Bancroft Library, UCB)

Index

Alexander, Wallace M., 28
American Stevedore Company, 81, 83, 94, 123
Anderson, Capt. A.E., 33
Anderson, Frank B., 27
Argonaut, 29–31
Armes, George, 68, 72
Ashe, E. Porter, 50, 121

Bentley, R.I., 115
Berkman, Alexander, 4, 31, 36–40, 43, 44–5, 49, 77, 113, 114, 117
Boardman, George, 21

Calhoun, Patrick, 11, 12, 102, 105
Castle, Walter, 68, 72
Chase, H. Van Rensselar, 90
Chipman, Minor, 116
Citizens Alliance, 13
Committee of Citizens, 120
Committee of One Hundred, 45–7
Crocker, William H., 57–9

Densmore Report, 128
Dollar, Capt. Robert, 27, 75, 96
Durney, Joseph, 68, 72, 75
Dutton, Rev. C.S.S., 66, 115

Employees' Liberty League, 42, 45
Employer's Alliance, 8, 13
Ernst, Hugo, 60–1

Fee, Grant, 83
Fickert, Charles M., 12, 106, 107, 108
Fogan, James J., 21

Hale, Marshall, 68, 72
Hanna, Edward J., Archbishop, 51, 52, 43, 65, 69, 96
Herrin, William F., 12

Hogue, S. Fred, 104
Hughes, Charles Evans, 54–64

Johnson, C.R., 28
Johnson, Hiram, 12, 56, 63–4

Kean, John, 18
Keesling, Francis B., 57–64
King, L.M., 21
Koster, Frederick J., 3, 21, 24, 25, 27, 28, 29, 32, 45, 46, 48, 51, 52, 66, 94, 103, 104, 108, 109, 112, 114, 123, 129, 130

Lynch, Robert Newton, 21

McBean, Atholl, 123
McDevitt, William, 4, 13, 40, 43, 60, 67–80, 96, 102, 125, 128
McNear, Seward B., 21
Mahany, Rowland G., 18
Merchants and Manufacturers Alliance, 13, 14
Metson, Drew & McKenzie, 28, 50, 53, 72–80
Metson, William ("Hell Fire Bill," "Billy"), 28
Michaels, C.F., 28, 115
Michel, William, 87, 117–8
Minor, Robert, 114
Mooney-Billings Affair, 11, 13, 39, 47–8, 60, 77, 79, 99, 106, 107, 109, 113, 125, 128
Mullaly, Thornwell, 41, 43

Nauman, Howard, 68, 72

O'Connell, John A., 49
Older, Fremont, 4, 11, 12, 31, 43, 47, 109

153

Oxman, Frank, 107

Phelan, James D., 11, 62

Rastall, Dr. B.M., 115
Reardon, F.A., 92
Rigall, F.E., 107
Rolph, George M., 28
Rolph, James R., Jr., 4, 13, 24, 32, 41, 45, 47, 51, 52, 53, 68–80, 86, 87, 90, 91–4, 96, 97, 100, 102, 104, 105, 106, 111, 112, 129–30
Rowell, Chester A., 32, 57

San Francisco Board of Supervisors, 111
San Francisco Center, 120
Scharrenberg, Paul, 43, 74–5
Schwerin, R.P., 18

Smith, Rev. Paul, 65
Spooner, William A., 43
Spreckles, Rudolph, 11, 43, 62, 78, 118
Sproule, William, 27, 51
Sullivan, Matthew I., 103–6, 118

Teller, Philip S., 27
Thackara, R.C., 18
Tveitmoe, O.A., 43

United Railroads, 99–106, 111, 113

Webster, Hugh M., 28
Welch, Martin F., 71, 73–80
Wickersham Report, 128
Wilson, William B., 19
Wittman, George, 92
Wright, Allan G., 94